INT
TRANQUILITY

A Guide to Seated Meditation

FINDHORN PRESS

Other Books by Darren Main

Yoga and the Path of the Urban Mystic

Spiritual Journeys along the Yellow Brick Road

Hearts & Minds:
Talking to Christians about Homosexuality

INNER TRANQUILITY

A Guide to Seated Meditation

DARREN MAIN

FINDHORN PRESS

© Darren Main 2003, 2010

The right of Darren Main to be identified as the author
of this work has been asserted by him in accordance with
the Copyright, Designs and Patents Act 1998.

Published in 2010 by Findhorn Press, Scotland.
This is a revised edition of *The Findhorn Book of Meditation*
published by Findhorn Press in 2003.

ISBN 978-1-84409-503-2

A CIP record for this title is available from the British Library.

Edited by Sue Louiseau, proofread by Nicky Leach
Cover and all photographs by Jasper Trout
Interior design by Damian Keenan
Printed and bound in the USA

1 2 3 4 5 6 7 8 9 17 16 15 14 13 12 11 10

Published by
Findhorn Press
117-121 High Street,
Forres IV36 1AB,
Scotland, UK

t +44 (0)1309 690582
f +44 (0)131 777 2711
e info@findhornpress.com
www.findhornpress.com

Dedicated to
SUE LOUISEAU
in honor of her tireless editing efforts,
and
for always returning to the breath.

Contents

Preface 9

Introduction 11

Part One - Learning How to Meditate 19

1 Learning to Sit 21

2 Training the Mind 33

3 The Obstacles to Stillness 41

Part Two - How Meditation Works 59

4 The Psychology of Meditation 61

5 The Physiology of Meditation 69

6 Meditation and Emotions 83

7 The Group Mind 93

Conclusion 111

Frequently Asked Questions 115

Styles of Meditation 119

Meditation Props and Supplies 121

Acknowledgments 123

Preface

In 2003 Findhorn Press asked me to write a book about meditation to be included in a series of books they were publishing on modern spirituality. "The Findhorn Book of…" series gathered inspirational spiritual teachers from a variety of traditions to offer basic "how-to" books that would inspire people new to the spiritual path as well as those who had been exploring spirituality for some time.

With that in mind, I set out to write a book that I hoped would inspire people to meditate on a daily basis. I hoped to offer them easy-to-understand tips for working through the inevitable obstacles all people experience when they attempt to quiet the mind.

All authors hope their books will sell and speak to a wide audience, but I was taken aback by the e-mails and letters I received expressing gratitude for *The Findhorn Book of Meditation* and how it had helped them not only to learn to meditate but also to develop a strong regular practice. Many had read other books on meditation and taken various courses, but maintaining a consistent practice remained elusive until they put into practice the simple techniques offered in *The Findhorn Book of Meditation.*

When the time came to reprint the book, I sat in a small café in Berkeley with my publisher Thierry Bogliolo and shared with him the feedback I had received over the years. I also expressed my desire to add more content to this edition and to expand its scope well beyond the narrow focus that was required in the original series of books. He enthusiastically agreed, and with that *The Findhorn Book of Meditation* evolved into the book you are holding right now. Because the scope of the new edition was more extensive than books in the original series called for, we decided to re-release the book with a new title and new cover to complement the greatly expanded content.

Inner Tranquility offers additional meditation techniques, more detailed explanations, a number of helpful photos, and many more resources to support you in your meditation practice. I have also grown as a teacher, a writer, and most of all, in my own meditation practice, and those insights are also present in *Inner Tranquility*.

For those of you who have read *The Findhorn Book of Meditation,* I hope you will find the additions in this book helpful in deepening your existing meditation practice. For those of you reading this work for the first time, I hope you will be inspired to begin a regular practice of meditation and that you will enjoy the benefits of having a quiet mind, an open heart, and a more balanced body.

Darren Main
February 2010
www.darrenmain.com

Introduction

What is before you is it, utterly whole,
complete and perfect.
To seek outside is to miss it totally:
This is a place you can't get to by going anywhere.
When we let go of all our battles and open our heart
to whatever is present, we come to rest fully
in the here and now.
This is the beginning and end of spiritual practice.
—*JACK KORNFIELD*

Like most children who were raised in a Western culture, I was not taught meditation. Although I was born into a Roman Catholic family, my personal inquiries into spiritual matters didn't begin until, as a young adult, I chose to look within for my happiness.

It was in 1989 that I began my spiritual path. At the time, I didn't even know what a spiritual path was or where it would lead, but the circumstances of my life had become so uncomfortable that change or death had become my only choices. I was at that proverbial fork in the road.

Although I was only 18 years old, my body was in sad shape. My muscles hurt, and I often suffered from stomach upsets, abdominal cramps, and migraine headaches. Advil and antacids had become staples.

This should not have come as a big surprise since I was living on coffee, fast food, and cigarettes. I was also getting by on as little sleep as possible, figuring that I could nap during my high school classes. Although my body appeared to be in good shape in as much as I was not overweight, I could not walk up a flight of stairs without becoming out of breath.

Emotionally and mentally I was in even worse shape. I found myself in frequent bouts of depression that seemed to last for months. Drugs and alcohol were the only things I could find that would bring me any relief from the dismal pit that my young life had become.

And so by fate, luck, or providence, I found myself in an Alcoholics Anonymous meeting—again. It was not my first meeting, but it might as well have been. My desperation and suffering had bottomed in an abyss that forced me to look at the 12-step program with fresh eyes. Although the 12 steps still seemed quite foreign to me, my ever-increasing level of suffering made them seem more and more palatable. They were starting to make sense for the first time. That is, all except for the 11th step.[1]

Step 11 instructs the alcoholic to create a daily practice of prayer and meditation. My aversion to the word prayer was not my biggest problem with this step. Though tight knots formed in my stomach whenever the word was mentioned, prayer was at least familiar to me.

Meditation was completely alien. Its very mention conjured up images of an old guru with a shaggy beard and a loincloth, sitting on a mountaintop. So I did what any good 12-stepper would do—I asked my sponsor. Unfortunately, he was not much help. He simply tossed out a few cliché AA slogans like "let go and let God" and "keep it simple." Unsatisfied, I started asking others at meetings but got a similar litany of answers.

And so I sought other venues. I tried self-hypnosis tapes and guided

---

1   Step Eleven: We sought through prayer and meditation to improve our conscious contact with God, as we understand him.

relaxation classes. I went to seminars at new age bookstores and even tried sitting with my eyes closed, waiting for something to happen. I didn't know what I was looking for, but I knew I wasn't finding it.

Fate has a way of putting in your path the things that you most need to find, and I eventually found a meditation group less than five miles from where I lived. It was a small group, composed entirely of women in their forties. It wasn't what I had envisioned, but I was grateful to have found it.

So every Tuesday night I found myself sitting in a circle chanting "Om" with a bunch of women, any one of whom could have been my mother. There was little that I had in common with the other members of the group, but a deep bond was formed nonetheless.

The glue that held this group together was its facilitator, Ellie. Ellie's gentle manner and compassionate eyes demonstrated to the group what was possible through the practice of meditation. Nothing seemed to shock or upset her. By contrast, my life was one upset after another. Ellie demonstrated that a mindful and centered life was possible and actually gave me the tools and techniques to realize those qualities in myself.

As I began my regular meditation practice, my lifestyle began to change. Within a year, I had quit smoking, cleaned up my diet, and started to regulate my sleeping habits. But more than this, my attitude changed. Much of my anger and bitterness toward life began to evaporate, and my relationships became much more civil and better adjusted.

My meditation practice, along with yoga, has now become the centerpiece of my life. They remain as much a part of my daily routine as brushing my teeth.

Several weeks ago, one of my new yoga students stayed after class to ask a few questions. She was about 18 or 19 years of age and was looking at me with the same sense of awe as I had once looked at Ellie. Although she was young, it was easy to sense her blossoming commitment to a spiritual life.

"You never seem to be upset," she said. "With all that meditation and yoga, you probably never get angry or upset. It must be nice."

I smiled, because I could hear myself saying those same things to Ellie years before. "I do feel anger and get upset just like everyone. The only difference is that underneath all the ups and downs that life throws my way there is a sense of peace. Emotions like anger and fear still come up. I just don't lose my inner peace quite so easily when they do."

That is what meditation is all about. I have come to believe that learning to quiet the mind and sit in stillness is the greatest gift people can offer themselves.

About This Book

Meditation is quite universal. In one form or another it has been practiced by every culture and religion on Earth. It was promoted by the Buddha, Krishna, Jesus, and Mohammed. Countless sages, shamans, and healers have been touting this diverse yet universal practice since before the dawn of history.

In fact, our busy modern world is one of the only cultures throughout history that has not placed a noticeable emphasis on spiritual introspection. Sure, many of us attend a church or synagogue—and these activities often bring with them many spiritual benefits. But learning to quiet one's own mind takes us beyond the lofty principles discussed in worship services and makes them real and meaningful throughout the week.

In the past, entertainment was scarce—at least by today's standards. In the nature of things, people had more downtime, and some form of meditation was part of daily life. This is not to say that most people lived like Buddhist monks—they certainly did not—but people did have more quiet time to contemplate who they were and what it was that they wanted out of life.

In our modern world, it is not easy to find some quiet amid the mobile phones and traffic jams. But through the rediscovery of meditation our society can become whole again, and we as individuals can enjoy life more. Really, we have two choices: either we learn to quiet the mind and find contentment and completion within, or we can keep skipping from one thing to the next, hoping that the new car or the new lover will be the answer to our unrest.

In this book, I hope to bring back to light some of the wisdom and practices known to our ancestors. We don't need to abandon our modern lives to implement these techniques; we just need to make a little space for them. Meditation can be every bit as useful today as it was in years past. Some would argue that it is needed now more than ever.

This book provides an overview of various aspects of meditation. It is designed to give a basic understanding both of how to meditate and why meditation is so effective at bringing us a more peaceful experience of life.

I divided this book into two parts. Part One concerns itself with learning how to meditate. From the basics of finding a seated position that supports your practice to exploring techniques that bring the mind back under control, this section of the book will give you the essential tools needed to start your practice.

In Part Two we will explore the mechanics of meditation. It can be very supportive to understand how meditation works and what the process actually looks like. On the surface, meditation can look as if you are sitting around doing nothing. In this section, we look at the effects of meditation at the psychological, physical, and emotional levels. We will also explore the effects of meditation on groups. Because we are all connected at the deepest level of our being, the practice of meditation offers great opportunities for any group of people who practice together—whether that be a husband and wife seeking to deepen their marriage or the whole human race becoming more peaceful and enlightened as more people find that state of inner balance. In the context of human relationships, meditation is a powerful vehicle for bringing about healing.

It is important to note that meditation is not a religion or a replacement for religion. You can have strong roots in any faith and still benefit from the practice of meditation. In fact, many people find that their own faith deepens as a result of practicing mindfulness. Therefore, you can use these techniques in conjunction with your religion or you can use them as a means to find your own unique relationship with the spiritual.

However you choose to use this book, it is my hope that you will make it personal and unique for you. Meditation is a very individual practice; if you learn to cultivate a practice that is tailored for you and your life, you will find limitless rewards.

This book is a guide to developing your own meditation practice. It is nothing more than that. There are many wonderful classes and meditation groups out there that will also support you in this inward pursuit, and there are a number of other books that teach a variety of meditation techniques emanating from various cultural and religious points of view. Exploring these other avenues will complement the information contained in this book.

Thirty Days

Meditation is a very simple practice. In fact, when people take my "Introduction to Meditation" workshop, they are often surprised at just how simple the practice is. The most difficult aspect of meditation lies in the commitment to do it daily. This is by far the biggest obstacle to developing a regular and rewarding practice.

For this reason, I ask new students to make a one-month commitment to practice daily for at least 20 minutes. This brings several important advantages. First, they gain a month's experience with meditation. During that month, the student has the opportunity to evaluate the practice and begin to feel its many benefits over time. Also, without a regular practice, a student can rely only on my word, or the word of other meditation teachers. Blind faith may be enough to get a person started, but it will not be enough to maintain a regular practice.

A month devoted to daily practice will also provide students with the opportunity to form good habits. Meditation should be like any daily habit. Taking care of the mind is every bit as important as taking care of the body. Using this first month to develop good habits will move the practice into the same realm as eating, brushing your teeth, and the like. Once the habit is firmly established, taking the time to meditate will become less of a chore and more and more a normal part of your day.

To that end, find a time to sit each day. Whenever possible make it at the same time and in the same place in order to use the mind's predilection toward ritual and habit to your advantage. In the pages that follow, you will learn how to sit and a few meditation techniques to get you started. By employing those techniques in regular daily practice, you will move them out of the realm of theory and into the far more potent realm of sustained direct experience.

If you were to take up swimming, gymnastics, dance, or singing you would not expect to master the skill on the first try. It would take time, but with regular practice it would become more natural. Meditation is no different, so take a moment now to make a firm commitment to 30 days of practice. At the end of 30 days you can make another month-long commitment if you like, but for the moment, one month is all that's required.

Darren Main
www.darrenmain.com

PART ONE

Learning How to Meditate

Truth is within ourselves;
it takes no rise from outward things whatever you may believe.
There is an inmost center in us all,
where truth abides in fullness; and around,
wall upon wall, the gross flesh hems it in,
this perfect, clear perception—which is truth.

— ROBERT BROWNING

CHAPTER 1

Learning to Sit

You do not need to leave your room.
Remain sitting at your table and listen.
Do not even listen, simply wait.
Do not even wait, be quite still and solitary.
The world will freely offer itself to you to be unmasked,
it has no choice. It will roll in ecstasy at your feet.

—*FRANZ KAFKA*

When I first learned to meditate, I was under the impression that meditation was easy—that it was some kind of relaxation exercise that would leave my body feeling as refreshed as after a gentle nap on a summer afternoon. This was the first in a rather long string of illusions that I held about meditation. It was an illusion that ended with about as much grace as a sparrow flying into a plate glass window.

At my first meditation class with Ellie, I had expected to sit comfortably while my mind drifted off to some magical and quiet place. I was excited about leaving my rather uncomfortable body behind for a bit, and I could feel a soft bounce in my step as I walked up the sidewalk to her yoga studio. *Learning to meditate was going to be just what I needed to overcome the discomfort that was my life.*

After some brief introductions and a short overview on how to meditate, we sat in a circle, around some candles in the center, and began the practice. All went well for the first minute or two. It wasn't what I expected, of course. There were no bolts of lightning, and the voice of

God didn't come booming down from the clouds. Nevertheless, I was sitting quietly.

Then I felt something very unexpected. My foot began to fall asleep. "Not a problem," I thought. "It will pass." No such luck. The pins and needles didn't stop. In fact, they got worse. They traveled up my legs until I cracked open my eyes to see if my feet had turned blue. Thankfully they had not. But while my eyes were open, I took a glance around the room. Everyone looked like a stone statue of the Buddha—still, quiet, and anchored in peace.

I closed my eyes again and felt the numbness begin to subside. "Now I will get to the good stuff," I thought. But the numbness only gave way to aching hips, a sore back, and knees that felt as if there were shards of glass inside them. On top of all that, my head hurt from trying to ignore the agony of my body. I was just about to get up and walk out of the room when I heard Ellie's voice coaxing us out of meditation.

After the meditation, each person had a chance to share. All of them seemed to have had a positive experience. One woman even cried a bit because she had found such a peaceful state. I could understand wanting to cry too, but peace was the farthest thing from my mind! Even though I had shifted positions, I still felt as if someone had taken a razor strap to my low back.

When it was my turn to share, I didn't know what to say. I had obviously done something wrong. Both my mind and my body were in complete hell. I decided to be honest rather than pretend. After all, I didn't plan on coming back, so I had no reason to lie. "Well, first off, I don't know what you folks did to make your meditation so wonderful, but I hated it. My body has never felt worse, and my mind feels like an animal chasing its own tail. Either I did something really wrong, or you are all masochists."

Ellie smiled and quietly let me finish my tirade before she responded. "Darren, meditation is not an easy practice, and sitting still is not easy for most of us. In the West, we are not encouraged to sit and go within for our answers. In fact, we are not encouraged to sit still at all. Our minds will resist this process—especially in the beginning stages of our practice. But if you are patient, you will work through many of these seemingly insurmountable obstacles."

There was something about her calmness that reassured me. She also showed me some ways to sit that would be less challenging to my body. I decided to give it another shot and came back the following week. That was the start of a new relationship with my body and my mind. Sitting can be difficult at times, even after years of meditation, but in general it has become much easier with regular practice.

In this first chapter, I will address some of the physical issues that come up when we meditate. The good news is that many of the techniques and suggestions I offer in this chapter will help alleviate much of the discomfort that I experienced during that first meditation. However, one point needs to be stressed: although there are many things you can do to make yourself more comfortable, a certain amount of discomfort is to be expected; in fact, that discomfort is part of the practice. Know that, as your practice progresses, sitting will become easier. The key to success is not to give up.

How to Sit

For seated meditation, there is only one rule that needs to be observed: keep the spine straight. Everything else is merely a suggestion that you can use or dismiss as you see fit. Slouching, lounging, lying down, and leaning are all the kiss of death to a strong meditation practice. Therefore, learning to sit in a comfortable upright position is paramount to a rewarding and long-term practice.

Try this little experiment. Sit in a nice tall upright position. Feel your spine lengthen and lift your chest a bit. Notice how that feels.

Your mind and your body are very connected, so it is fundamental to put your body in a position that says "attention." Now try slouching. Round your shoulders forward and let your head hang. A position such as this is likely to evoke drowsiness and invite your mind to wander. Lying down, while perfect for relaxation and sleep, will make the practice of meditation very difficult.

REMINDER

Meditation is a time to focus, train the mind, and bring it to stillness. It is not a time to rest and relax.

Because it is so important to sit upright, there are several preferred positions. As far as meditation is concerned, all of them are effective, so try to find the position that works best for you. Learning to sit on the floor rather than on a chair has its advantages, but don't feel that it is a requirement.

THE LOTUS POSE: About a year ago, I was teaching a meditation class to a group of fifth graders. They were very excited to be learning just about anything other than math and English. I started the class the way I start many of my meditation workshops—by asking the group what they knew about meditation.

Immediately a bunch of hands went up, and I called on an enthusiastic boy in the front row who was so sure of himself he looked as if he was about to jump out of his skin. No sooner did I call on him than he hopped out of his seat, sat on the floor, and wrapped one leg over the other. He then closed his eyes and started making the sound of "Om." Naturally all the students laughed and started "Om-ing" right along with him.

What he was doing was not meditation itself, but a popular sitting pose called lotus. This pose is perfect for sitting, as it tips the pelvis slightly forward, which encourages the spine to be straight and tall. This gives greater support to the spine and back, and you can sit longer with less discomfort.

Unfortunately there is a little catch. If you have injured knees or tight hips, it will be extremely painful, if not impossible, to sit in lotus. This is where hatha yoga really supports a meditation practice. By working to keep the hips and legs open, hatha yoga makes the lotus posture much more accessible. To learn this pose, I recommend consulting an experienced hatha yoga teacher in order to avoid injury.

The Lotus Pose

HALF LOTUS POSE: Because most of us don't start a meditation practice until adulthood, there is a good chance that our hips and knees will be too tight for the lotus. Therefore, most people need to use a meditation cushion and a modified pose called the half lotus.

In the half lotus pose, your legs stack one on top of the other. This provides some of the same benefits as the full lotus, but allows you to open your hips more slowly. The effects are not quite as dramatic, but it is a much more realistic alternative for most people living in Western cultures.

Because the half lotus is modified, most people need additional support. This is where a meditation cushion is helpful. The cushion should not be too soft—in fact, the firmer the better. There are a number of stores and yoga studios that sell cushions designed for sitting. (See Appendix C.) You can also use a firm, folded blanket.

Proper placement of the cushion or blanket is very important. Rather than sit on it with the back of the legs as you would sit on a chair, you will want to sit so that your buttocks are on the cushion and your legs are on the floor. This will help to tilt the pelvis forward and will encourage that straight spine.

The Half Lotus Pose

> **TIP**
>
> Take some hatha yoga classes. The practice of hatha yoga was designed to help people sit in meditation for long periods of time. In addition to its many physical benefits, hatha yoga is sure to make your meditation practice a lot more comfortable.

CHAIRS AND BENCHES Sitting on the floor with legs crossed can be a very grounding experience and can be a wonderful part of your practice. However, if you spend your whole time in agony, you will have a very short meditation career. For some people, sitting with crossed legs is simply not an option, and other means are suggested.

One option is a meditation bench. These benches are designed to take most pressure off the knees while encouraging the spine to remain straight. They can be easily built or ordered from a number of companies. There are also a number of Web sites[2] that provide building instructions, which can further reduce costs. (See Appendix C.)

Sitting on these benches is simple enough. From a kneeling position, place the bench behind you, above your calves. Now sit back, placing your buttocks on the bench. I find it helpful to put some padding under the knees as well. A blanket folded several times works quite well.

For some people, especially senior citizens, getting on the floor is not an option. In these cases, I suggest using a straight-backed chair. This allows for a straight spine and an alert mind without the problem of getting up and down. The important detail here lies in the choice of chairs. Something like a couch or lazy boy would not be very supportive.

---

2   http://www.embody.co.uk/blog/post/how_to_make_a_meditation_stool

Although these types of chairs are well suited for watching television or taking a nap, they tend to keep the mind in a less than focused state. It's best to choose a chair that is firm and has a straight back. Also, try to choose something that will allow the feet to be planted firmly on the floor.

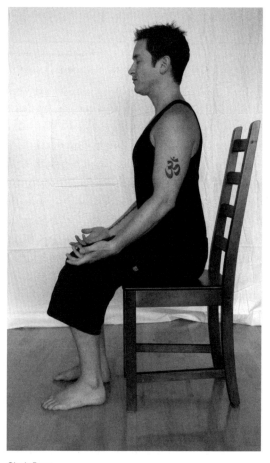

Chair Pose

Time

When learning to sit in meditation, we need to think about timing. There are two basic questions that need to be answered before we can proceed. The first one is, how long will I meditate today? And the second, when will I meditate?

Regular meditation is much more effective than sporadic sits, even if those sits are longer. In other words, you will experience more benefit from sitting for 15 minutes every day than from sitting for one hour once or twice a week.

Therefore, it is important to decide when you will meditate and for how long. For myself, I prefer meditating first thing in the morning. This has two benefits. First, it starts my day off on the right foot. This doesn't guarantee a great day, but I have found there is a definite correlation between the days that I start with meditation and the days that seem to run more smoothly. I have also found that meditating first thing insures that I make the time to sit. I am much more likely to forget to meditate if I try to make time for it later in my day.

Of course, not everyone is a morning person. Some people prefer to meditate on their lunch break or just before dinner. One thing most people find helpful is to make meditation part of a regular routine. One way to do this is to meditate at the same time each day.

Tools for Timing

HOME PRACTICE SERIES: To help you time your meditations I have recorded a meditation home practice guide designed with this book in mind, and available for download on iTunes, Amazon, and other services. On the recording I gently guide you into the meditation, from time to time remind you to return to your breath or mantra, and then guide you out of the meditation at the end of 20 minutes. Consequently, this is also helpful as a timer for your practice.

IPHONE MEDITATION TIMER: Simple Touch Software [3] has a great App for the iPhone and iPod touch called *Meditator*. It allows you to time your meditations without clock watching and brings you in and out of the meditative state with a variety of sounds, including Japanese flute, chanting monks, and singing bowls.

When Not to Meditate
After a large meal
Just before bed
After drinking caffeine

Good Times to Meditate
First thing in the morning
Before meals
Several hours before bed

The other thing to consider about timing is how long you choose to sit. I would recommend sitting for at least 15 minutes. Short meditations of 10 minutes or less are not without benefits, but to really start getting into the deeper realms of the mind, a minimum of 15 minutes or more is necessary.

Of course, it is preferable to sit for longer than 15 minutes. In fact, I encourage my new meditation students to sit for 20 minutes, and my more advanced students to sit for 30 minutes or more. Meditation is a lot like cardiovascular exercise. Just as you need to do a minimum amount of time to shift the body into aerobic mode, and every minute

---

3   www.simpletouchsoftware.com

past the minimum you burn more calories, the mind works the same way. Every minute you spend in meditation after that initial 15 minutes takes you deeper and deeper into the unconscious mind.

The important thing is that you choose an amount of time that you can commit to. Deciding to meditate for 45 minutes each day is great, but if you only pay lip service to it, you are not doing yourself any favors. You will benefit more by choosing a shorter period of time, such as 20 minutes, and doing it consistently than by having lofty intentions and never actualizing those ideals in your life.

TIP

To time yourself, take a small clock or watch and place it on the floor in front of you. Before you close your eyes to meditate, look at the time and figure out the time when your meditation will be over, e.g., when the big hand is on the four and the small hand is 20 minutes past. This saves you from having to do math while you are trying to meditate.

Once you start your meditation, you can peek from time to time to see how much longer you have. After a while, you will have to peek less and less, but in the beginning this can be a helpful way to make sure your meditations start and end on time. Another option is to find a timer with a very gentle bell. You don't want to be jolted out of your meditation.

Although we have covered a lot of information about how to sit, we have still not discussed the actual practice of meditation. Everything we have covered in this chapter is a foundation for what is to come in the rest of the book.

CHAPTER 2

Training the Mind

It is very hard for people to understand
what it means to have a silent mind.
They immediately conclude that such a mind has
"No thoughts, no thoughts at all."
Truly speaking, a quiet mind is a mind with patience.
You do not need to root out all thoughts.
Some thoughts are quite sacred: they take you to God.
So, having a silent mind does not mean
erasing the light of the mind.
A silent mind, a still mind, has patience.

— *GURUMAYI CHIDVILASANAND*

On one of my retreats to Costa Rica a few years back, I decided to offer the students a basic meditation workshop. Whenever I lead this workshop, I like to survey the group to see how much they know about meditation and what misconceptions they may have about the practice. It is also helpful to know what people hope to get from the workshop.

One man said this in response to my inquiry: "Being on this retreat has been great; I feel better than I have felt in a long time. The one thing I haven't been able to do is get my mind to shut off completely. I am hoping that you will give me a meditation technique that will allow me to turn off my mind whenever I want to."

The other students nodded and smiled in agreement. I had to chuckle to myself because I knew exactly what he meant. When I first started meditating, I was looking for the right technique or a sacred mantra to undo the years of craziness that existed in my mind. I knew there had to be a technique out there that would work for me—something that would end the madness of my mind once and for all.

Unfortunately for me, for the people on that retreat, and for anyone who has ever tried meditation, there is no magic pill. There is no one technique that is easy and foolproof, and there is no fairy godmother who will tap you on the head with the wand of enlightenment. The realization that meditation is work—lots of work—is the first thing that we need to address before we can look at the practice itself.

Think about it. You have probably spent your whole life believing that thoughts are just something that happen to you. If you are like most people, you have been feeling like a victim of those thoughts when they make you unhappy and like royalty when they make you feel good.

The mind and all its thoughts seem to be happening accidentally because we have let the mind get out of shape and become undisciplined. We have countless ways to entertain the mind and distract it from boredom. We have any number of ways to justify our thoughts and the emotions and actions that inevitably follow those thoughts. And we have become masters of projection—pushing the responsibility for our own thoughts outward so that the consequences of our thoughts become someone else's problem.

We have done this for years. Our untrained minds have deep habitual grooves carved into them—grooves that desperately need to be sanded down and retrained through the practice of meditation. However, doing this is not going to be easy. These mental habits and patterns are sure to trip us up and distract us over and over again as we practice.

TIP

No matter how many times you get distracted during your meditation, RETURN to the practice. Everyone gets distracted all the time. It is the nature of the ego mind (see Chapter Three) to get distracted. The practice of meditation involves realizing you have become distracted and then returning to the practice without judgment. It serves no purpose to beat yourself up for becoming distracted.

Now in the case of the man who attended the meditation workshop in Costa Rica, I had to break the bad news to him. He was disappointed that I wasn't going to offer him an easy way out of his busy mind, and so were many of the other students in the class, but there was a positive side. While meditation is not an easy out, it is a very effective way to train the mind. Although it is a lot of work, it is a lot less work than letting the mind run amok. The good news is that the mind can be trained and brought under control.

The other day I was sitting in the park with my laptop, writing the introduction to this book. There was a woman walking her dog, or I should say, the dog was walking her. She was a small woman, and her dog was rather large. The leash was pulled tight and her time was spent screaming obscenities at the dog and trying to manage its unruly desire to chase other dogs, bark at strangers, and mark every tree it could find.

The scene was quite funny, but what really completed the picture was another woman who came walking up behind her. She also had a dog, but her dog followed her. It was not on a leash and didn't need to be. This woman spent her time playing with her pet. She threw a tennis ball and wrestled with her dog in the grass.

This is the choice we make when we start meditation. We are choosing to train the mind. Rather than letting the mind drag us through life on a leash, the mind becomes our friend and companion. Just as a puppy can be trained to follow you and sit when you tell it, the mind can also be trained. But discipline and commitment are needed. Dogs don't magically become well behaved, and neither do minds. Just as training a puppy takes practice and can be a lot of work, so training the mind is not always easy and the commitment to the training process is long term. However, the benefits of taking control of the mind will affect every aspect of your life.

Types of Meditation

Whenever I say that I teach meditation, everyone seems to ask, "What kind of meditation do you teach?" This is an understandable question because there are hundreds or thousands of different meditation techniques. Some of them are connected to religious traditions while others are more secular.

In general, all meditation techniques fall into one of four categories. Understanding these basic categories will help you ultimately pick a style of meditation that is best suited for you. Let's look at each of these categories in turn.

JAPA MEDITATIONS: The word *mantra* comes from the Sanskrit language, which is broken into two syllables—*man* (mind) and *tra* (tool or instrument). Thus mantra literally means "instrument of thought" or "mind tool." Most often, however, it is translated as "sacred sound" or "sacred word." The practice of japa is the repetition of a mantra or prayer. Although the words *mantra* and *japa* come from the East, the repetition of a mantra or prayer is not confined to Eastern traditions.

The purpose of japa is to help keep the mind focused and open the practitioner to deeper states of awareness. Your mantra can be in an ancient language like Hebrew, Latin, or Sanskrit, or it can be a more modern word such as "love" or "peace." A few examples of mantra meditations include Transcendental Meditation, the use of mala beads by Hindus and Buddhists, and the Christian practice of the Rosary.

CONTEMPLATIVE MEDITATIONS: A great way to train the mind is to keep it focused on a concept or idea. In our world of bright and sexy images, it is not easy to focus on the deeper meaning of a riddle or scriptural passage, but that is what the contemplative traditions ask of their students. Generally speaking, a student of this style of meditation chooses (or is given) a concept on which to reflect. This can be anything from a paradoxical question to a passage from a religious text. Examples of contemplative meditation include Zen koans, Jana yoga, and Christian Centering Prayer.

VISUALIZATION MEDITATIONS: One way to keep the mind focused is to hold an image in the mind's eye. For people who tend to be more visual, this can be a very useful technique. Some people will envision something simple, such as a candle flame or a religious symbol. Other people will visualize the image of a saint, guru, or deity. Visualization meditations should not be confused with hypnosis or guided visualizations. There is a distinct and well-defined difference. Visualization meditation is about focusing the mind on a single and relatively unchanging image. Guided visualizations and hypnosis generally keep the mind very active and often involve an ever-changing narration. This is not to say that the guided experience is not helpful; indeed, for many people it can be profoundly helpful. But it is not a substitute for a regular meditation practice.

BODY-CENTERED MEDITATIONS: The nice thing about the body is that it is always in the present moment. This means that bringing the focus to the body is a quick and effective way to focus the mind. Also, body-centered meditations are usually neutral in respect to religious beliefs, so they are a bit easier to integrate into your own individual beliefs. Some styles of body-centered meditation focus on the breath while others focus on sensations in the body. Some even focus on movement. Styles of body-centered meditation include hatha yoga, Tai Chi, martial arts, and Vipassana (insight) meditation.

Techniques to Get You Started

As I have mentioned, there are countless styles of meditation. I would like to teach you two of my personal favorites, which you can use to get started. You may find that these techniques are perfectly suited to you and you may choose to use one of them for years to come, or you may find another technique that works better for you. If that is the case, I encourage you to use that technique instead.

The Buddha was once asked which meditation technique was the most effective. The master's response was both simple and profound: "The one you practice." So, start your practice with one of these simple techniques and explore others as well. The important thing is that you get started and that you practice consistently.

ANAPANA – MEDITATION ON THE BREATH: Sit in a comfortable upright position. Some people sit cross-legged, others prefer to kneel. It is also acceptable to sit in a straight-backed chair (see Chapter One). Allow your body to relax and take a few deep, full breaths to shift into a quiet space.

As you begin to quiet down, focus on the sensation of the breath as it flows in and out of the nose where it touches the upper lip. There is no need to change the quality of the breath. Simply watch it move in and out. You will find that the mind will frequently wander. This is natural. Once you notice that the mind has wandered, gently bring it back to the breath.

The whole process is one of bringing the mind back to the breath over and over again. Try not to be discouraged by how much the mind will wander. You have been letting your mind wander undisciplined for many years. You can't expect it to sit still overnight. Rather than chastising yourself for letting your mind wander, praise yourself for noticing, and gently bring it back.

JAPAANAPANA – MEDITATION ON A MANTRA: Sit in a comfortable upright position. Some people sit cross-legged, others prefer to kneel. It is also acceptable to sit in a straight-backed chair (see Chapter One). Allow your body to relax and take a few deep, full breaths to shift into a quiet space.

As you begin to quiet down, begin repeating your mantra. My favorite mantra is Om Shanti. As you inhale, silently say "Om" (the sound of creation). As you exhale, silently say "shanti" (peace). Each time your mind wanders—and it may be often—simply return to the mantra. Try not to dwell on the fact that your mind became distracted; simply return to your mantra over and over again.

If "Om Shanti" doesn't resonate with you, there are many other mantras from which to choose. Here are just a few from various traditions:

Mantra	Inhale	Exhale	Tradition
Thy will be done (Matthew 6:10)	"Thy Will"	"Be Done"	Christian
Here I Am (Exodus 3:4)	"Here"	"I Am"	Jewish
Mother Goddess-Father God	"Mother Goddess"	"Father God"	Pagan/Wiccan
Allaahu Akbar (Call to Prayer)	"Allaahu"	"Akbar"	Islam
Hong Sau	"Hong"	"Sau"	Yogic

Before moving on to the next chapter, I recommend that you sit and meditate for at least 20 minutes and start to develop a daily practice. This will give you a point of reference as we look at meditation in more detail.

CHAPTER 3

The Obstacles to Stillness

The one who has entered a solitary place,
whose mind is calm and who sees the way,
to that one comes insight and Truth
and rapturous joy transcending any other.

—DHAMMAPADA

In the previous chapter we looked at some of the basic types of meditation that are available and learned a few simple techniques for getting started. Now we are going to refine our skills even further. If you have started your meditation practice, as suggested at the end of Chapter Two, you have no doubt realized that it is much more difficult than you might have expected. In this chapter we are going to look at the very things that make the practice difficult and provide you with some practical tips for dealing with these distractions.

When I first began my meditation practice I thought I was crazy. I would sit to meditate and my mind wouldn't be still. All I had to do was one simple thing: watch the breath. But my mind would twist and turn, like a cat trying to avoid a bath. I wondered what was wrong with me. I thought for sure that I was completely insane and that no one else could possibly be as disturbed as I was.

What I have learned through my years of practice, and even more through my teaching, is that I am by no means unique. Everyone struggles with meditation. Everyone feels as if they are ready for an insane asylum. The games that the mind plays to keep us distracted are not unique, either. One would think that, with the vast capacity of the human brain, there would be thousands of ways to keep us distracted when, in fact, there are only five. Once we learn these five "mind games," we can begin to see through them and take back control of the mind.

Before we learn to handle these five obstacles, however, it is helpful to understand a few things about the mind itself. We are going to be covering the psychology of the mind in a later chapter, but for now we will be content to ask the question, "Who am I?"

Practice Session

Sit with your eyes closed for a minute or two and consider the question, "Who am I?" Feel free to make a list in your head of the things that define you. Statements such as "I am a mother" or "I am an accountant" are likely to fill your head. Most of your answers, however, will not be WHO you are. These false beliefs about yourself are part of a spiritual identity crisis called the ego.

As human beings, we have two identities. One is real, and the other is an illusion. As odd as this may sound, it is quite true. The real Self (usually written with a capital "S") is the part of the mind that exists in a natural state of peace—a constant state of knowing that doesn't become upset and turbulent. This is the part of the mind with which we are seeking to connect more deeply through the practice of meditation.

This true Self is not identified by the details of one's life. Things like jobs, relationships, and recreation can be expressions of this true Self but are never to be confused with it. The Self stands on its own and is complete without external or finite labels.

The false self is commonly referred to as the ego, and could not be more different. The ego defines itself by its judgments and stories. It believes it *is* the experiences it has had in life *and* the judgments it holds about those experiences. Its core belief is that it is separate and small. It feels, and rightly so, that if it lets its guard down for even a second, the vastness of the true Self would eclipse it. Therefore, the ego has a vested interest in keeping the mind busy. When we sit still in meditation, we begin to quiet the ego mind and start to listen to the true Self. To our egos, this is the most dangerous thing we can do.

In light of this, we can easily see why the ego struggles to keep the mind busy. When we sit still, the ego is not happy. In fact it is downright upset. That is why it has devised the five obstacles I am about to teach you. These five obstacles are very clever tricks, but with a little mindfulness they can be understood. Our ego uses these tricks when we are living our day-to-day lives, but they don't really become evident until we try to quiet the mind.

REMINDER

The ego mind exists because of the constant churnings of thought that it creates. If you are struggling to quiet the mind during meditation, you can be sure it is because the ego senses you are close to realizing something important. That's when the ego decides to kick up some dust. The best thing you can do in these situations is stay committed to your practice.

Craving

In the West, we live in great material abundance. Pleasures to stimulate every sense abound at every corner. We have movies filled with special effects to give us eye candy, and stereos to massage our ears. Food has become much more about flavor, and its function to support and nourish the body is often overlooked. While there is nothing innately wrong with enjoying the pleasurable aspects of life, it can become burdensome—especially when you are trying to meditate.

It is important to note that natural instincts such as our appetite and our sex drive guide us and help preserve our health and survival. These "appetites" are normal and natural; however, the ego will distort those impulses and use them for its own goals. Some examples of the ego's warped impulses are overeating, acting out sexually, and any number of other destructive behaviors.

As we live our lives, it is important to learn to distinguish between an ego craving and a natural body appetite. If we get confused between the two, as many of us often do, trouble is sure to follow. In normal life it is not always easy, learning to distinguish between a craving and an appetite. But in meditation practice you can be sure that what you're feeling is almost always craving.

If you were to sit for 20 or 30 minutes or even an hour, it is unlikely that you would have any real biological needs except for oxygen. Food, water, sex, and the other natural body appetites can safely be put on hold for much more than an hour. Therefore, it is almost always inappropriate to give in to a craving when you are meditating.

Our ego mind loves pleasurable things. It seeks them out all day long, and when we close our eyes to meditate those cravings don't stop. In fact, those cravings can intensify because we are not catering to them.

When we sit and meditate, cravings are one of the key ways that the ego mind keeps us distracted. Because for most of us, it is such a pattern in our lives to satisfy our cravings, the ego simply extends this pattern into our meditation practice. For me in the beginning, it was one of the most effective ways the ego had of pulling me away from my breath.

This morning when I sat to meditate, I could feel my mind spinning out of control with cravings. First, I wanted to see what was on the news. I was sure something major was happening. More than anything I wanted to get up and turn on one of those cable news stations. I resisted that craving, however, and did my best to return to my breath. Then I had a thought. What if I am right? I could prove that meditation has made me more psychic if I just get up and turn on the television. After all, it would be done in the name of my practice. I continued with this line of thinking for almost five minutes, and I almost convinced myself to end my practice early, just so I could satisfy my craving for the news.

My experience this morning was not unlike the ones you will probably have as you practice. Of course you may not have a craving for news. It may be for a snack or some other sensual pleasure. It may not even be for something that involves getting up. It may be enough for your ego to keep you in a dialogue about the thing you are craving. Cravings can be very strong. In fact, many people find them overwhelming. That is why it is so important not to give in to them.

It is also very important to learn to deal with them. A meditation practice doesn't require us to suffer. But it does ask us to resist temptation. The ego would love nothing more than to have us run to the refrigerator or turn on the news. It knows that once we do so, the meditation is over and it gets to keep its job.

Therefore, in the context of your meditation practice, the only way to deal with craving is not to give in to it. As I mentioned above, the only thing we really need for the length of our practice is oxygen. Everything else can wait. Once you give in to that craving, the ego will know what works. It's like trying to teach a dog not to beg and then feeding it scraps of food under the table. You are teaching your ego that cravings will distract you and, knowing what an effective tool they are, it will use cravings all the time.

It is usually pretty difficult to resist cravings. But there are a few concrete things you can do to help address the cravings as they arise.

ACKNOWLEDGE THE CRAVING: If you are craving food simply say, "Craving food." Look at it for what it is. Once you realize that it is an ego game, it will become that much easier to return to the breath. The cravings may go away once you acknowledge them, or they may not. But whatever happens, you will be better prepared to stop yourself from acting on them.

AVOID MOVING INTO FANTASY: We will discuss fantasy later in this chapter as it is one of the other obstacles, but it can work hand in hand with craving. If you are craving a piece of chocolate cake, letting the mind run wild with a fantasy about how great it will taste is only going to make matters worse. If you find yourself going down that road, be sure to acknowledge what you are doing and return to the breath.

GIVE YOURSELF PERMISSION: Assuming you are craving something that will not hurt you, give yourself permission to work through the craving after your meditation. When I wanted to see what was happening in the world. I gave myself permission to turn on the television after my practice. This was very helpful in letting me return to the breath. Interestingly, I no longer wanted to turn on the news when I had finished. This often happens with cravings that come up during a practice.

DON'T STOP UNTIL YOUR TIME IS UP: If you cut your meditation short because of your cravings, the ego has won. You may not be able to spend much time with the breath and you may be very uncomfortable, but if you get up and cater to the ego's cravings, it will only make your next meditation more difficult.

TIP

Cravings will come up during your meditation practice. There is nothing wrong with experiencing cravings. The important thing is not to give in to them. If you do, you will only invite more.

Aversion

Just as the ego would have you spend a lot of time looking for pleasure and has a short list of cravings that it loves to engage in, so it also has a strong desire to avoid the uncomfortable. This ego practice is called aversion. Like its cousin craving, aversion shows up in life and acts even more vigorously when we come to the meditation cushion.

Backing away from pain is not necessarily a bad thing. It is a very natural part of our survival instinct. For example, if you were to stick your big toe into a tub full of hot water, you would naturally pull your foot back to protect yourself. If you didn't have this basic instinct, you would jump into the water and your whole body would be scalded.

Just as the ego takes the body's natural appetites and exploits them to create cravings, so it creates aversions by exploiting our natural resistance to physical pain. An aversion is based on the same principle as resistance to pain, but it is not real. In fact, it can oftentimes cause more pain than was actually avoided.

Divorce is a difficult process. I don't know anyone who has enjoyed the experience. It is certainly not something one would look forward to, but it is, at times, necessary. This was the case with my parents. They were married for 25 years and had some good times, of course, but much of their marriage was strained. Both of them knew it wasn't working. Neither spoke to the other about it, nor ever showed any verbal or physical affection. In addition, neither seemed to want to work on improving the marriage.

My parents lived with each other in a constant state of suffering, but neither wanted to walk though the uncomfortable process of divorce. This is a classic example of aversion. My mother finally did ask my father for a divorce, and it was not easy for either of them. Letting go of the past and wondering about the future during midlife must have been very challenging, but in this case it was for the best. When the ego uses aversion, it convinces us that because something is difficult or uncomfortable it must be dangerous and should be avoided.

I had a similar experience when I gave up smoking. Quitting smoking is one of the most difficult and uncomfortable things a person can do. Of course, not quitting will ultimately make for an even more uncomfortable situation. The ego, however, doesn't look at the big picture. That is why it took me several years of trying before I was actually able to quit. The ego had me focused on the discomfort of the moment rather than the bigger picture.

When we sit and meditate, the ego will use the full force of this aversion principle. The ego loves to create stories about why it is better to get up and do something else rather than meditate. If it can't convince you to stop the meditation altogether, then it will settle for busying the mind with all sorts of entertaining stories. In either case, when you find yourself in aversion mode, you are very likely close to a breakthrough. Just as was true of craving, the key is not to give in—in this case to the desire to avoid. Here are a few things you can do that may help you resist aversion:

ACKNOWLEDGE THAT YOU ARE IN AVERSION MODE: This may sound odd, but sometimes just acknowledging it can bring you back to the breath.

REMIND YOURSELF THAT YOU ARE SAFE: When you are sitting in meditation, there is no waiting tub of scalding water and nothing to be afraid of. Therefore, whatever comes up is a game the ego is playing.

DON'T GIVE IN TO THE AVERSION: If you do, the ego will use it all the time.

Dealing with aversion is not easy. The things that come up can seem very real and can be very uncomfortable. But like giving up cigarettes, the benefit of not catering to the aversion is well worth the effort. On the other side of that discomfort is liberation from the ego's bondage.

Agitation

Back when I was trying to quit smoking, aversion was not the only thing that came up. Agitation was right up there, too. I call this the pacing tiger syndrome. It is something like aversion, in that it feels very uncomfortable, but it carries a more general sense of discomfort, one that you can't put your finger on. You don't know what you want. Whereas aversion and craving are associated with a definite need or desire, agitation is not. In many ways this makes it more difficult to address.

Agitation is not something you can pinpoint. It is a feeling of unease, a discomfort with the current situation but with no solution at hand. It's like standing with a growling stomach in front of the refrigerator door and not knowing what you want to eat.

The ego loves agitation because it generally results in a person hopping around like a madman who has just stubbed his toe.

When we are on the meditation cushion, agitation is bound to come up. For me personally, it is my ego's favorite game. There is no one thing that I want to do. I just don't want to be where I am. I also find myself fidgeting a lot. For me, agitation often comes with the sensation of a tickle or scratch someplace on my body. Of course, as soon as I break down and scratch it, my ego creates another and another until I am in a virtual seizure, scratching myself and adjusting my position.

Dealing with agitation is not going to be easy, and I wish I could say that I have a simple and easy way to get around it. Unfortunately, I don't. What I do have are a few pieces of advice on how to address agitation when it comes up.

ACKNOWLEDGE THE AGITATION: If its origin is apparent, you can acknowledge that as well. Like the previous two obstacles, you can often make agitation drift away by simply shining the light of awareness on it.

MAKE SUBTLE ADJUSTMENTS TO YOUR POSTURE: Be very mindful not to let the ego take you for a ride. Sometimes it's better to sit with a modest amount of physical discomfort than to let the ego lead you through a gymnastic routine during your meditation.

DON'T CATER TO YOUR AGITATION: If you give your ego its way and get up before the appointed time, you will find that agitation will visit most of your meditations, and you will never be free. If you can stick it out, you will find that agitation will be your companion less and less often.

I can't stress enough that it won't be easy to get around agitation. Like the other obstacles to your peace of mind, it creates even more difficulties if you don't deal with it as it comes up. Remember that what we experience during our meditation practice is a model of how we interact with life. If we can learn to face our agitations on the meditation cushion, we will find that our reactions to life itself will become more centered and peaceful.

Fantasy

The other day I found myself half asleep in the shower, thinking about a run-in I had with one of the guests at a book signing at a small town in the central valley of California. A few conservative "Christians" had decided it was their job to come to my talk about yoga and inform me that I was teaching "the devil's dance." They were friendly enough with their assertions, but their comments were certainly out of line.

Ever since my first book was released and I started putting myself in the public eye, I have encountered people like this—folks who disagree with me and feel the need to tell me so while I am standing in front of a crowd with a microphone in hand. I have learned to acknowledge them and their opinions and then move back to my own talk. This usually pacifies them.

In this case, the people in question were very upset because a friend of theirs had found yoga and rarely went to church with them anymore. This, of course, fueled their "devil's dance" perception. Although our interactions were brief, I found that I was left with a feeling of incompletion because they had walked out while I was in mid-sentence.

So when I found myself in the shower, half-asleep, it was all too easy to drift into fantasy mode. I would rehash the scenario over and over, changing details and thinking about the things I could have said or done differently. In some of the fantasies they stuck around and decided to take up yoga. In others they left, but I had a very clever quip as they walked out the door.

Of course, none of it mattered because it was not what had actually happened. It wasn't until the shower started to run cold and I had to rinse the conditioner out of my hair, polar bear style, that I was able to break free from my ego's fantasy world.

Fantasy is something we do all the time, but mostly on an unconscious level. The ego is a master storyteller, and it loves to hear itself speak. Its stories have nothing to do with reality. In fact, they have everything to do with preventing a person from seeing reality.

These fantasies can be nice, or they can be ugly. They can be somewhat realistic, or they can be completely far-fetched. From a meditation point of view it doesn't really matter. The ego uses fantasy to keep the mind busy in unreality. Rather than be in the present moment, which is the only place where reality can be experienced, the ego would have us living in the future or the past.

We can clearly see how this is played out in real life. You can fantasize about becoming a writer, or an actor, or making a difference in the world. But all the fantasies ever dreamed up have not been enough to make that become a reality. *Sculpting the future and healing the past can only happen through action in the present moment.*

When we meditate we seek to ground the mind in the present moment. We focus on the breath or the image of a saint or a mantra. All this is designed to keep the mind present, so we can choose to let go of past baggage and our attachments to what the future should hold. The ego doesn't like this, so it uses fantasy to lure the mind out of the present moment.

I have found that when I will not give in to craving, aversion, and agitation, the ego smiles and says "Okay, you won't end this meditation, so I will keep your mind busy until it is over. Have fun…." Make no mistake about it: avoiding fantasy is not easy. Even when you realize it is a fantasy, the temptation to engage in it remains powerful. Choosing to disengage from a fantasy can be extremely difficult. Here are some suggestions on how to deal with fantasy when it comes up.

ACKNOWLEDGE THE FANTASY: Some fantasies will be pleasant; others would land you in jail if you acted them out. Whatever the fantasy, acknowledge that it is not real and return to the breath.

DON'T JUDGE YOURSELF: When you realize you are in the midst of a fantasy, don't waste time judging it. Many fantasies have a very strong pull. Even if you manage to return to the breath or mantra once, you may find yourself back in the middle of the fantasy over and over again. Try not to judge yourself for this. Instead, simply return to the breath over and over again.

TRY TO AVOID THE MEDIA JUST BEFORE MEDITATING *(television, news, and the Internet):* Its only effect will be to provide the ego with fantasy material. There is nothing more enjoyable than arguing religion and politics when you don't have a real opponent to argue back.

REMEMBER, FANTASIES ARE NOT REAL: Always remember that your fantasies are not real and they don't deserve your attention.

Sloth

The last trick the ego uses to distract us, both in life and meditation practice, is sloth. Sloth can take many forms: emotional depression, mental sluggishness, physical fatigue, and so on.

Sometimes these feelings have legitimate biological causes. For instance, some forms of depression are organic (caused by a chemical imbalance in the brain); and a person will certainly be physically tired at the end of a long day of heavy labor. However, many times sloth has nothing to do with these legitimate circumstances and is, in fact, manufactured by the ego.

Have you ever spent a day doing nothing and found at the end that you were more tired than on days when you were highly productive? This is the ego at work. Sloth is not about physical, emotional, or mental fatigue. Sloth is about the ego telling the mind to go to sleep.

Learning to spot the difference between sloth and genuine fatigue is key. Both natural fatigue and depression, as well as the sloth manufactured by the ego, can interfere with your meditation practice. However, each must be dealt with in different ways.

Let's look at the non–ego-based fatigue first. As we mentioned, this can manifest itself on all three levels: mental, emotional, and physical. The best way to deal with this natural form of fatigue is through lifestyle changes. There are a number of things we can do. Here are a few:

- Wake up at the same time every day.
- Go to sleep at the same time every night.
- Avoid caffeine (even in the morning).
- Sleep six to eight hours EVERY night.
- Avoid oversleeping (too much sleep is just as bad as not enough).
- Don't meditate just before bed.
- Give yourself enough time to wake up before a morning meditation.
- Don't lie down to meditate.
- For organic depression and mental lethargy the following tips may help:
  - Avoid refined sugars.
  - Be sure to exercise regularly.
  - Get the right amount of sleep each night.
  - Avoid meat and foods high in fats.
  - See an herbalist for suggested herbs.
- If none of the above helps, see a doctor.

While these lifestyle suggestions are sure to make your time sitting on the cushion easier, they are not directly connected to meditation. However, observing some or all of the above suggestions will make the identification and management of ego-based sloth much easier. It is difficult enough to deal with ego-based sloth by itself. If you are feeling depressed or are overtired, it will be a real uphill battle.

When my ego uses sloth to distract me from my meditation, I sometimes find my mind wandering into a dreamlike state. Soon I find my head nodding and my posture slumping. This ego game is especially difficult because I am half-asleep for the whole thing. Needless to say, my mind is far from my breath, and I would much rather go to bed than sit in meditation.

In dealing with sloth on the meditation cushion, the first step is to choose times to meditate when you will not be tired before you start. For example, after a heavy meal or just before bed are not the best times. Choose times when you are not likely to want a nap. Before meals tends to be best for most people.

Second, if you find yourself getting drowsy, try shifting positions and deepening the breath a bit. This can snap you out of it and help bring a bit more oxygen to the brain. Many times, I find this enough to make me more alert and refocus my mind.

If all else fails, you can stand up to meditate. The eyes will remain closed and the focus will remain on the breath, but the body will need to keep the mind more alert to prevent you falling over. Eventually, you can sit back down. The ego usually tires of standing and will stop trying to put you to sleep when you return to a seated position. Here are a few additional suggestions.

TIP

- Finish your meditation—even if you feel like you are not getting anywhere.
- Never lie down to meditate.
- Don't use drugs such as caffeine to keep you awake or you will find yourself dealing with the agitation instead.
- Wash your hands and face before meditation. This can make you feel more refreshed.

The above obstacles are not easy to overcome, but the suggestions I have listed will make it simpler. The key is awareness. Once we recognize the ego's games, they become that much easier to avoid. The first time you walk down the path you may trip over a stump, but once you know it is there, you will be less likely to fall. You may trip from time to time when you are not paying attention, but acknowledging the pitfalls will go a long way toward avoiding them.

The next step in learning to meditate is to identify these obstacles as they appear and continuing to return to the breath in spite of them. By acknowledging these distractions we train the mind to become more vigilant toward them, and as we do this we trip over them less and less. This is a great benefit in your meditation practice and an even bigger benefit in life.

Practice Session

From now on when you meditate, try to identify the obstacle that distracts you. As you find your mind somewhere other than the breath or mantra, say to yourself "craving," "aversion," "fantasy," or "sloth," and then gently refocus. This will prove a great tool, both for bringing the mind back and also for recognizing the distraction.

PART TWO

How Meditation Works

*The art of archery is to draw the arrow
back on the bow as far as possible and
then to release the arrow, sending it ahead
with great force.*

*Likewise, the mind should be drawn back
to the source of thinking and, from there,
released to bring the thought out in a more
forceful manner supplemented by
the power of the Being.*

*It will bring out a powerful thought
that will succeed in the relative world,
bring the infusion of the Being
into outside activity, and make possible
the state of cosmic consciousness.*

— MAHARISHI MAHESH YOGI

CHAPTER 4

The Psychology of Meditation

*Pure silence is within you. It is not just the absence of sound,
or lack of noise. It is the ground, the basis of your very being.
There is nothing to find out, nothing to get, nothing to prove.
Just listen with your whole being to what is here, now.
It is the most amazing thing you can ever discover.
It is with you now. It is you.
The only way to find this is to stop everything else.
Everything! Just be!*

—*MARK MCCLOSKEY* [1]

To fully appreciate the practice of meditation, it is very helpful to understand exactly what we are doing and why we are doing it. As a child, I found it maddening that adults would tell me to do something without any explanation as to why. When pressed for a reason, I would frequently hear the well-known response, "Because I said so."

Unfortunately, many religious and spiritual traditions have taken the same attitude. They encourage a contemplative life involving prayer and meditation, but have done little to explain why it is so important. Therefore, in this chapter and those that follow, I would like to explore the "why" of meditation. As we have already noted, meditation has some very noteworthy benefits, but the richness of the practice is greatly

---

1 www.puresilence.org

enhanced when the mechanics of the mind are more fully explored and understood.

I believe that meditation is a powerful and useful tool, and explaining how it works can only encourage its regular use in our daily lives. So let us start with what I call the anatomy of the psyche. The psyche is the part of the mind that is conscious, though as we shall see, not all aspects of consciousness are necessarily part of our awareness. In fact, much of the mind is very unaware of itself, which is one of the major reasons why meditation is so important.

As I write this, I am sitting in Golden Gate Park in San Francisco. It is a beautiful September day, and the lawn and gardens are lush and full. There are many tiny flowers in the grass around my blanket, and an attractive woman is jogging by. Not a bad moment. In fact, I would put it right up there on the list of great moments this week.

Everything I have just described is part of the first level of consciousness, which I call the "Conscious Mind." It is the part of the mind that is most familiar to us because that's where we spend most of our day. This is the level of consciousness where information about the world outside enters our psyche and is, for better or worse, judged.

Now the more weight we give to a certain judgment, the deeper that judgment sinks into the mind. We will talk more about judgments in a moment, but for now, let's just focus on the fact that we judge. Most experiences are judged, and it is the conscious level of the psyche that begins the process of filing those judgments in the nether regions of the unconscious.

The tiny sliver of the mind that is our conscious awareness seems to be all there is, but we know this is not the case. We dream at night, and while awake we make unconscious Freudian slips. We have episodes of déjà vu, and we make many life decisions without consciously knowing why. The unconscious mind is a vast territory, which for most of us is largely unexplored.

So let's take a look at the mind with its several levels and start to understand the anatomy of the psyche. I generally divide the mind into four basic parts. The lines between these levels of consciousness are blurry at times, but it can be helpful to think of them as distinct and separate parts.

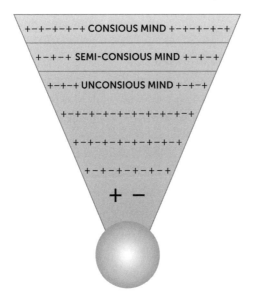

Unified Field

The deepest level of an individual's mind is what Einstein called the Unified Field (UF). Basically, if you go deep enough into anything in the physical universe (including the human mind), you arrive at the same point. This point has been called many things over the years, but its nature is universally accepted to be an experience of joy and bliss. Some people call it the Promised Land. Others call it Samadhi or Nirvana.

The followers of Jesus were instructed to seek the Kingdom of Heaven "within" themselves.[2]

The important thing is not what we call this Unified Field but rather where it is. The great mystics of the past would not have us look for it at the mall or even in a church pew. Rather, they would have us look deep within. This is meditation's ultimate goal.

The Semiconscious and Unconscious Mind

We have already spoken about the conscious mind, but what of the other parts? Let's start with the semiconscious mind. This level of our consciousness is what we experience in daydreams and REM (Rapid Eye Movement) sleep. We can often recall some of our daydreams and our dreams while we sleep, but at best they tend to be hazy, and many details are missing.

That is because this level of the mind is only partially conscious. Our daydreams and our fantasies have an otherworldly quality that lives just below the surface of our conscious awareness. Even though we may have some control over these dreamlike images, they tend to have a life of their own. There seems to be little choice in how we experience these images.

It is even more difficult to pin down the unconscious mind. While the images and dreams that we experience at the semiconscious level are sometimes far fetched, they at least resemble our daily lives. They are linear in nature and seem to follow most of the rules (albeit loosely) of the physical universe.

However, the unconscious mind follows its own set of rules. It is nonlinear, and its content can often seem bizarre and illogical. Maybe it will be a fleeting image or a shape. Perhaps it will be a sound or a voice.

---

2   Luke 17:21

These unconscious thoughts are sometimes beautiful and sometimes disturbing. One thing is certain, however: we spend so little time there in a conscious way that this deep level of the mind is almost always foreign to us.

Bending Spoons

So we have a mind with several parts: the conscious mind at the surface; the semiconscious and unconscious minds below that; and finally our source point, the unified field.

When we spoke about the unified field, or source point, you learned that this is the part of the mind characterized by joy and bliss. These are two very desirable qualities, but we see them so rarely in the world. There is a very good reason for that. In spite of the fact that each of us has at our core the qualities of joy and bliss, in between we have three levels of mind filled with judgments.

If we didn't judge, that source would radiate joy and bliss through our mind to be easily expressed in the world. But most of us hold vast numbers of judgments that bend and warp our true nature into something that looks very different.

You see, every experience you have ever had—the big ones and the small ones, too—has been judged by your ego. Some things are judged to be negative and others to be positive. In either case, the ego places a little kink in the mind. Then, when the light of pure joy and bliss shines through it, it gets bent and distorted in the same way that a prism breaks light apart.

The goal of meditation is to remove these judgments so that more and more of our lives can be an expression of that joy and bliss. This, of course, can be a daunting task. Removing all this mind clutter can feel a lot like cleaning out and organizing your teenage son's or daughter's room.

The Effect of Meditation on the Mind

So how do we do this? If the mind is filled with judgments and most of the mind is not even consciously available to us, then where do we begin? How do we begin to neutralize something we don't even know is there?

That is where meditation comes in. The whole practice of meditation is linked to raising awareness and neutralizing judgments along the way. As an example, let's look at my practice from one morning several years ago.

I started my practice the way many of us do—by sitting still and bringing my awareness to the breath. I had a busy day ahead of me, so I found myself drifting to thoughts of the day. There was an early morning meeting with a nonprofit group about a fund-raiser, and I had to catch a flight to Washington, DC. My mind kept rehashing the day and trying to plan it out. I realized this a number of times and each time, after acknowledging that I was in fantasy mode about my day, I returned to the breath. All these distractions were part of my conscious mind, and each time I decided to return my mind to the breath, these judgments lost some of their power over me.

Because I continued to return to the breath, the meditation technique took me a bit deeper and I reached the level of the semiconscious mind. Here I found myself in a daydream about bumping into [now former US president] George W. Bush at a cafe while in DC and inviting him to attend the yoga workshop I was about to teach. After finishing the class, he decided to spend the rest of his term in office fighting for world peace, environmental stability, and civil rights for all beings.

Now, as far fetched as that daydream might seem, it was very fun to engage in it. I realized several times that I was being distracted and tried to return to the breath, but it took a good 10 minutes before I could let the fantasy go. What was not quite so apparent was what lay behind this daydream. While it seemed harmless enough, behind it were the judgments held in my semiconscious mind. They had created the whole thing. By constantly returning to the breath, I was able to withdraw some of the energy from them. This allowed me to move into the unconscious mind.

As I moved into the unconscious mind, I found myself distracted by a number of images that were anything but normal. First, I saw my friend Christopher's head turn into a pumpkin with the standard jack-o'-lantern eyes and mouth. Strangely, it still looked like him. Then he reached up and pulled the top off his pumpkin head and a white mouse holding a pumpkin seed scurried out and scampered off. I was quite amused at first, but quickly realized that I needed to return to my breath. Then I got distracted again. I started to wonder what that odd image meant. I labeled this distraction as a form of craving and moved back to my breath. I was starting to go into another image when I realized that it was time to end my meditation.

This morning, I did not get deep enough in my meditation to experience the Unified Field, although I have visited it in the past. That was all right with me, though. It was enough that I had been able to let go of a number of judgments and return to the breath quite a few times. My mind was more still than when I had started, and I felt ready to move forward into my busy day.

This is how meditation starts to reshape the way we think. We can use it to move beneath the surface of our minds and choose again. Most people spend their lives feeling like victims of luck or fate. This is because their most important decisions are made on an unconscious level.

By clearing the mind through meditation, we allow more of our decisions to be made consciously, which exponentially improves our personal lives and the quality of the communities of which we are a part.

Points to Remember

All thought radiates from one central point. This source is known by many names, such as The Unified Field, God, The Great Spirit, The Tao, Allah, and many others.

The mind is divided into three basic levels:

- *Conscious mind* experienced as conscious thought
- *Semiconscious mind* experienced as dreams and fantasy
- *Unconscious mind* experienced as archetypes and symbols

Our perception, to a large extent, and the world we live in, are the products of our judgments. These judgments can be either positive or negative.

An individual's collective judgments create an ego, which is the perception that the self is small, isolated, and finite.

CHAPTER 5

The Physiology
of Meditation

Having tasted the sweetness of inner solitude and calmness,
the one who lives by the Law is free from fear and suffering.
It is joy to see such awakened ones, and to live with them in happiness.
To travel with the unawakened makes the journey
long and hard and is as painful as traveling with an enemy.
But the company of the wise is as pleasant as meeting with friends.
Follow the wise, the intelligent, and the awakened.
Follow them as the moon follows the path of the stars.

— *DHAMAPADA*

In the West over the past few years, meditation has caught on like wildfire, due in large part to its extraordinary physical benefits. Although the masters and teachers of meditation have long maintained that its physical benefits are a small fraction of the spiritual and psychological benefits, it is hard to ignore its healing effects on the body.

What was once seen as a weird activity reserved for hippies and mountaintop gurus is now becoming so popular that my Health Maintenance Organization (HMO) has a poster advertising a meditation class for people with heart disease. Opinion has come full circle, due largely to numerous studies printed in peer-reviewed medical journals.

In addition, medical doctors such as Dean Ornish, Bernie Siegel, Herbert Benson, and Deepak Chopra have sought to integrate meditation into Western medicine. Thanks to these pioneers, we no longer have to choose between Western medicine and Eastern meditation. The two are being more and more tightly integrated. The mind-body connection is not only being acknowledged but is also being used to treat illnesses from AIDS to cancer to heart disease, with well-documented success.

Understanding the physiology of meditation is not essential. It will work for us whether we understand it or not. However, this understanding can help deepen our commitment to the practice and can also help us to work more consciously with the mind-body connection.

A New Field of Study

In 1975, Herbert Benson, MD published his now classic book, *The Relaxation Response,*[1] which sent shockwaves though the medical community. Benson, a cardiologist, noticed a distinct trend among his patients with high blood pressure: stress.

Initially he did what most doctors did at that time (and to a large extent still do today). He prescribed medications designed to lower blood pressure. While these drugs frequently had the desired effect, they often carried with them annoying side effects.

Benson began to investigate natural ways of reducing blood pressure by looking for ways to reduce the stress that so often accompanies hypertension. This led him to the Transcendental Meditation movement (TM), founded by Maharishi Mahesh Yogi, which was seeking researchers who would validate their claims of improved health.

In 1969, Benson joined forces with a researcher named Robert Keith Wallace at the University of California to research the effects of this technique on physiology. Their research results were startling.

---

1   *The Relaxation Response* by Herbert Benson, M.D. with Miriam Z. Klipper, HarperCollins, 1975

Practitioners of Transcendental Meditation were able to reduce their heart rates, regulate blood pressure, and improve overall health.

Over time Benson studied other meditation techniques and found similar results, ultimately labeling this ability to shift one's physiology by regulating the mind, *The Relaxation Response.*

Today it is hard to imagine the revolutionary nature of Benson's research and book and the radical shift they created in the way medicine is practiced. While some would argue that we have not come nearly far enough, a major transformation occurred as a result of Benson's research. Today, many doctors openly embrace integrative medicine as a means of treating everything from anxiety to cancer to HIV, and Benson's book remains as relevant today as it was in 1975.

Stress and Pressure

Before we can understand how meditation affects the body, we need to understand stress and pressure, because it is stress that causes negative responses in the body.

We all face challenges in life. Of course, some days or months or years are better than others, but life can be difficult. We deal with difficulties at work, in our relationships, within our families, and with the deaths of people we love.

All these situations create what I call pressure. I call it pressure because it comes from outside of us. Pressure can come from many sources, but in all cases it creates a squeeze that can be difficult to process. Sometimes, even the best events in our lives can put pressure on us. A wedding or a job promotion can be just as intense as the loss of a job or a divorce. Pressure happens when the world outside demands our attention.

Stress is an internal response
to external pressure.

This is an important distinction. While pressure comes from outside us, and we have little control over it, stress is entirely an internal matter. Stress happens when the external situation becomes too overwhelming for the mind to process calmly, and we experience a change in our physiology as well as in our emotional and psychological selves.

We need to be able to distinguish the two because stress is often harmful to the body. We will cover more on that in a moment, but for now let's just focus on the difference between stress and pressure. Sometimes we can control the events in our lives and arrange its details so they produce less pressure, and we feel less stress as a result.

Unfortunately this is not always the case. Too often we have little say in what happens in life, and the pressure we experience can be overwhelming. This is why meditation is so important. Even though we can't control all the things that happen outside ourselves, through the practice of meditation we can control the stress response that happens within.

I had two friends, Michael and Jeff, who were lovers for more than 15 years. Jeff was diagnosed HIV+ about a year after they met and managed to live well for most of their relationship. He ate well, took his vitamins, and practiced meditation. In fact, he didn't even take medication for most of the time they were together.

About two years before he died, Jeff started on an aggressive treatment recommended by his doctor. This was quite effective in lowering his viral load [2] but, unfortunately, it affected his cholesterol level and his heart, and he died of a fatal heart attack.

Jeff and Michael had been through a lot together, and they used

---

2   A test used by some doctors to measure HIV. A low or undetectable viral load is thought by many doctors to prevent or delay the onset of AIDS.

Jeff's HIV status as a springboard from which to jump high and cel-ebrate life. Even though they had done a lot of spiritual work and had a lot of faith, Jeff's death hit Michael quite hard. He went into a deep depression, and his life started to unravel. Everything, from his job to his friendships, was deeply affected. Eventually he decided to take up yoga again.

After one of my classes we sat and chatted. It was amazing to see how much Jeff's death had affected Michael on a physical level. He was not just emotional; he had lost weight and his eyes looked tired. Even his hair looked unhealthy.

Michael was no stranger to meditation, and with a little coaxing he agreed to return to the daily practice that he and Jeff had shared each morning. It was about a month before I saw him again. What a differ-ence! He looked much better, and his eyes looked soft again. It was as if he had been drinking from the fountain of youth. I asked him how he was holding up, and he responded by saying, "It is tough; I miss him so much. I still cry myself to sleep every night, and that ache in my chest doesn't feel like it will ever leave. He was my best friend. But the meditation really helps. I still feel the pain, but I am no longer crippled by it. It washes through me rather than knocking me over."

There is nothing Michael can do to change the source of his pain. He can't bring Jeff back, and the grief of losing him is not likely to go away anytime soon. That event will continue to put pressure on Mi-chael for many years to come. While the source of Michael's pressure is beyond anyone's control, how he responds to Jeff's death is another story. Because stress is entirely internal, Michael has a choice, albeit a difficult one. How his mind responds to that pressure will determine how much stress he will experience, and in turn how his body will be affected.

Stress and the Nervous System

As we mentioned, Michael's stress had a very noticeable effect on his body. This is true of all stress, for all of us. Stress in the mind creates a very measurable effect in the body, and usually one that is undesirable.

The body has an autopilot system called the Autonomic Nervous System (ANS). The ANS is very important to our continued health and survival. It regulates many things that are beyond our conscious control, such as heart rate, breathing, digestion, and immune function. These all happen in the background with little or no effort on the part of the conscious mind: You don't need to remember to beat your heart; it just beats. Furthermore, if you decide to run around the block, your ANS will tell the heart to beat at a rate that is more appropriate for cardiovascular exercise.

The ANS has two subdivisions. One is responsible for what is known as "fight or flight [3]," and the other for "rest and digest [4]." Each of these has a very different but important function for our health and survival.

The fight-or-flight aspect of the ANS is responsible for getting us out of harm's way. It tells the heart to beat faster, the adrenal glands to produce adrenaline, and the blood to flow to the limbs. For example, if you were walking down the street and someone jumped out of an alleyway to mug you, your body would kick into fight-or-flight mode. This would give you the biological resources to fight off your attacker, or run to safety.

The rest-and-digest aspect of the nervous system is what manages the body's daily activities—things like digestion, elimination, immune response, and our resting heart rate.

---

3   Sympathetic Nervous System
4   Parasympathetic Nervous System

These two systems work well together for the most part: one gets us out of immediate danger, and the other helps the body to nourish and heal itself. They work together to help ensure a long and healthy life.

However, the system has one flaw. The ANS can't tell the difference between a real physical threat (e.g., a person jumping out of a dark alley) and psychological stress (e.g., getting audited by the IRS). Both physical threats and psychological stress are treated in the same way, with some very unfortunate results.

Because the ANS can't tell the difference between a person jumping out of an alley and an IRS audit, it responds to both by tightening the muscles, constricting the internal organs, and releasing adrenaline into the body. Together, these responses put the important rest-and-digest functions on hold.

There are several reasons why this is a problem. First, we were not designed to stay in fight-or-flight mode for any length of time. Most dangers do not continue for years. While the fight-or-flight mode may be an important and lifesaving part of our wiring, it is not a place where you want to spend much of your life. Unfortunately, many people are so stressed that they spend almost all their time there.

Second, the fight-or-flight mode only helps with physical danger. More adrenaline is not going to help with that tax audit or that difficult divorce. While those pressures may be the seeds of a lot of stress, they do not immediately threaten our safety. Addressing these situations from fight-or-flight mode is not only unhelpful but can actually make it more difficult to resolve the issues.

Third, the long-term effects of being in fight-or-flight mode are quite negative. Adrenaline may get you out of a dangerous situation, but it is very hard on the immune system. Constricting the organs may help protect them from attack, but it is not good to leave them that way for long. Digestion and elimination are impaired as well as the functioning of the kidneys and liver. Even the skeletal muscles will start to constrict, to be ready to fight or run. This is why many people get tight knots in their backs and shoulders.

Lastly, body and mind are very connected. If the body has posted a state of emergency, the mind has little choice but to follow. Remember, it is the stress in the mind that has created this physical state. It's ironic that the body's physical state will now worsen the psychological stress. It is a never-ending cycle that leads to more and more suffering, disease, and chronic pain. There's a great book called *Why Zebras Don't Get Ulcers* by Robert Sapolsky if you'd like more detail on this subject.

Change Your Mind, Heal Your Body

All this talk about the nervous system is great, but it's just talk if we don't learn how to manage our stress. If people live under constant stress, their physical health will surely pay a price. It may start as chronic headache or heartburn, but eventually it can become something much more serious.

Meditation is powerful medicine. The body is the servant of the mind. The body responds to virtually everything that the mind thinks. It doesn't matter what is real. If the mind thinks it, the body responds as if it were real.

When I was in high school, my mother woke me up in the middle of the night. She was visibly shaken, and I knew immediately that something was wrong.

My younger brother Jason was 16 at the time and had just received his driver's license. He was not in the house, and my mother's car was missing. There was no note, and it was well beyond his curfew.

My mother was sure that my brother had been in a car accident or that some other awful fate had befallen him. One hour turned into two, and still he did not come home. My mother was sick with fear. Her body looked like it had been hit by an emotional wrecking ball.

Then, just as she was about to call the police, my brother came home. It turned out that one of his friends had just split up with his girlfriend, and my brother had gone over to his house to make sure he was okay. Because it was late, he hadn't bothered to wake my mother to tell her.

The truth was that my brother was fine, but my mother's head wove all sorts of stories about what might have happened to him. As a result of the activity in her head, her body reacted as if the stories in her mind were real.

Most of us do this all day long. Our minds create stress, and that stress triggers a physical reaction that most often is inappropriate. Rather than keep the body calm and relaxed, this stress sends the body into a downward spiral of dis-ease and discomfort.

We break that cycle when we meditate. We stop telling stories about what is happening, and we allow the body and mind to find an appropriate response to outside pressures without creating a needless physiological response that does not solve the external problem and is actually harmful to our health.

The nice thing about the body is that it wants balance. If you walk into a hot room, the body will sweat to cool itself off. If you walk into a cold room, the body will shiver to create heat—all this to maintain a steady body temperature. The body wants to be balanced, in a state of homeostasis.

When we quiet the mind's stories through the practice of meditation, we allow the body to work its magic and find health. Until we quiet the mind, the body gets one mixed signal after another. Then health and balance become goals that seem always just out of reach.

Practice Session

Close your eyes and imagine you are in your kitchen. Notice its familiar sights and smells. Now see a cutting board and knife on the counter, with a large bowl of lemons on the side.

Take one of the lemons and cut it into pieces. Feel the juice and smell the lemon as you pick up a wedge and bite into it. Feel the lemon juice fill your mouth and slide down your throat.

Now open your eyes. Notice what has happened inside your mouth. Most people can create a physical change inside their mouths simply by thinking about eating a lemon. Just imagine how many things happen in your body all day long because of your conscious and unconscious thoughts.

Positive Effects of Meditation
on the Body

Most of us who were raised in the United States have been taught that if you aren't busy doing "stuff," then you are wasting your time. Then how can the practice of sitting in meditation be good for you? Let's take a look at the effects that meditation has on the physical body.

CARDIOVASCULAR AND RESPIRATORY SYSTEMS: We place a lot of emphasis on cardiovascular health here in the West. Heart disease, high blood pressure, and stroke are all among the top killers in developed nations. Most industrialized countries have done an adequate job of educating people about the dangers of a high fat diet and a sedentary life, but they have not done much to educate the public about the need to manage stress.

It is very important to eat well and exercise, but it can also be a major support to add meditation to the regime. Meditation has been shown to lower blood pressure and improve circulation. Some also believe that the heart needs rest as well as exercise. Meditation seems to provide this.

The lungs are also affected by meditation. Researchers are finding that simply to breathe is not enough for good health. Quality breathing, which takes in the right amount of oxygen, is deep and full. Meditation helps us slip into a state where our lungs are working at their peak.

DIGESTION AND ELIMINATION: We have all heard of people who have digestive problems as a result of stress. Many cases of ulcers, constipation, and diarrhea can be linked to stress. When the body is in fight or flight mode, the organs of digestion and elimination are hindered. They get less blood flow and are generally constricted. Meditation can help alleviate many problems in the gastrointestinal tract as well as in the liver, pancreas, kidneys, and other organs that support digestion and elimination.

Several years ago a woman came to my meditation workshop in a state of utter desperation. She had lived with Irritable Bowel Syndrome (IBS) for many years and had seen six different specialists and worked with a nutritionist. Her symptoms often included abdominal cramping and bloating, excessive flatulence, and bouts of both diarrhea and constipation.

She had tried a wide assortment of prescription drugs, herbal supplements and changes to her diet to heal the IBS, but nothing seemed to work. Finally, a very intuitive nurse suggested she try meditation to help her manage her stress.

Given that she had tried everything else, she figured she had nothing to lose. She enrolled in my workshop and shared with me privately about her condition. I explained to her that while there are many factors contributing to colon health, that stress was a major contributor to dysfunction in the colon and that for many, a regular meditation practice can help the colon and other organs of the gut to find balance.

She was so desperate that she was willing to try anything and made a commitment to my recommended 30 days of meditation. At the end of the 30 days, I received the sweetest e-mail from her thanking me for my support. Her symptoms had almost completely disappeared for the first time in many years, and while she also needed to maintain a mindful diet, she was convinced that her meditation practice was a major key to her recovery.

She is not alone. Over the years I have seen all sorts of gastrointestinal (GI) issues improve as a result of a regular meditation practice. Ulcers, colitis, Crohn's disease, and many other GI conditions have been shown to improve significantly by simply using meditation as a complement to a combination of natural and allopathic therapies.

IMMUNE SYSTEM: The connections among meditation, the immune system, and overall health is presently being studied in more detail. In fact, a whole new branch of medicine called psychoneuroimmunology is evolving. This is very exciting news, because science is starting to catch on to what mystics have known for thousands of years. More and more, the effects of meditation on the immune system are being scientifically demonstrated and documented in medical journals.

The study of the mind-body connection is a very new science, but the benefits of meditation and similar practices are becoming more and more clear. For its health promoting virtues alone, meditation is worth every ounce of effort, but as we shall see, that is only the beginning.

The Osher Center for Integrative Medicine in San Francisco has been at the cutting edge of mind-body research and treatment for both cancer and HIV/AIDS. In 2008, Dr. Kevin Barrows began an exhaustive study of HIV/AIDS patients who engaged in meditation on a daily basis to see if there was a measureable difference in viral load, CD4 and

CD8 counts, and overall health. While his research is still ongoing, his findings thus far have been quite impressive.

Similar research has been done on autoimmune diseases such as lupus, multiple sclerosis (MS), and chronic fatigue syndrome. Autoimmune diseases are conditions in which the patient's own immune system attacks the healthy tissues of his or her body. For example, in MS, the immune system attacks the protective myelin coating around the nerves causing the nerve impulses to "short out." This can lead to a loss of motor skills, paralysis, and even death. In many cases, regular meditation practice has proven effective in slowing disease progression, lessening the severity of symptoms, and in some cases repairing damage caused by the autoimmune disease.

CHAPTER 6

Meditation and Emotions

It is your thoughts alone that cause you pain.
Nothing external to your mind can hurt or
injure you in any way. There is no cause
beyond yourself that can reach down and bring
oppression. No one but yourself affects you. There
is nothing in the world that has the power to
make you ill or sad, or weak or frail.
But it is you who have the power to dominate all
things you see by merely recognizing what you
are. As you perceive the harmlessness in them,
they will accept your holy will as theirs. And
what was seen as fearful now becomes a source of
innocence and holiness.

—*A COURSE IN MIRACLES*

During many of the retreats I facilitate, we spend a lot of time in seated meditation. Every morning we have a two-hour practice, which includes an hour and half of hatha yoga and a half-hour of meditation. During one retreat a woman approached me. She seemed a bit distraught, so we went for a walk and found a nice seat overlooking a lush Costa Rican coffee field.

"My dream is to be a yoga teacher, but I don't think I am cut out for it," she said, tears filling her eyes. "I find myself crying almost every time I sit to meditate. I think there is something really wrong with me. I think I should leave the retreat now rather than waste any more of my time or yours."

I gave her a hug and reminded her to breathe. Once she had calmed down, I explained. "We are doing a lot of yoga and meditation. Part of this retreat is bringing you deep within, and sometimes what you find there are some pent-up emotions that need to come out. Not only are you okay, you are clearing out a lot of stuff. All those tears are cleansing you and bringing you to a deeper understanding of yourself. You are going to make a great yoga teacher, so hang in there."

In the beginning, most of us are quite shocked when emotions come up as a result of our meditation practice. A lot of us have the preconception that meditation will make us really peaceful and calm, and that sadness and anger will be a thing of the past once we start the practice. There is some truth to that in the sense that a regular practice usually leads to a more balanced emotional state, but you will probably need to work through a lot of suppressed emotions first. Working through them means feeling them, and that usually means shedding a few tears in the process.

If you develop a regular meditation practice, you can count on having an emotional release at some point. Of course, some people carry more buried emotions, and others are more emotional by their very nature, but I have yet to meet someone who meditates regularly and who has not had at least an occasional emotional release as a result of their practice.

It is very important to learn to understand these emotions and how to deal with them. We live in a culture that tells us that emotions are a bad thing and that when we feel them, we need to control them. For men, in particular, feeling emotions is frowned upon. Most of us tend to get uncomfortable when we see people cry, because we think it means that something is wrong.

Actually, this is a backward way of thinking. When we cry or laugh uncontrollably, we release intense waves of psychic energy. If this energy doesn't move, it builds pressure until there is no alternative but for it to come out in an inappropriate way. It is like damming a great river. The force of that river builds behind the dam. Eventually that energy needs to be released.

When we sit in meditatation, we start to release, in a safe way, the emotional pressure that has built up within. The nice thing about doing this in the context of a meditation practice is that we have the opportunity to experience release in a way that is less destructive than your average nervous breakdown.

> *Emotion: a mental state that arises spontaneously*
> *rather than through conscious effort and is often*
> *accompanied by physiological changes…*
> —*THE AMERICAN HERITAGE DICTIONARY*

Most emotions have several features or qualities in common. First, all emotions seem to be uncontrollable. In other words, they seem "to just happen," perhaps because of an event, a thought, or a memory. They may even occur as a result of a movie, book, or piece of music. In any event, they seem to have a life of their own. They rise and fall like waves on the ocean: some big, others small, but there is little we can do to control them.

I once had a roommate who was dating this great guy who was good-looking, had a great job, and was fun to be around. Everyone liked him. Perhaps that is why everyone was so surprised when my roommate ended their relationship. When I asked her why she would let such a great catch slip away, she said, "Jimmy is a great guy, and I care about him a lot. I just don't love him. I want to, but the feelings are just not there. I can't make myself love him."

She was so right. You can't force emotions. You can't make yourself feel something you don't. How you feel is how you feel. Of course, as we shall see, emotions are very fluid and are in constant flux.

The second important quality about emotions is that you can't make them go away. They are there, like it or not. We can deny them and pretend they don't exist. We can even suppress them and push them down into the nether regions of the unconscious. But eventually we need to deal with them—hopefully, in a healthy way.

Third, there is a fluid quality to emotions, so that their nature is ever changing. This is a very important aspect, especially when it comes to meditation. The fact that they are always changing means that if you sit with an emotion, it will eventually change. Where I grew up, there is an old saying: "If you don't like New England weather, just wait a minute, it will change." The same is true of emotions.

A fourth feature of emotions is that there are really only two, love and fear. Of course, there seem to be many more. We can easily point to fits of anger and bouts of jealousy. We can remember times of great joy and contentment. But all the varied emotions we seem to feel have their roots in only two. The first, love, originates in the part of our mind that is connected to Spirit. It is the source of all the different types of love, which include peace, joy, happiness, and a whole bunch of other "positive" emotions.

The other root emotion, fear, is always inspired by the thinking of the ego. It gives birth to anger, jealousy, rage, depression, and all of the "negative" emotions. If we were to trace our emotions back and really look at them, we would see that they can all be traced back to love or fear. Take, for example, jealousy. If we really think about it, the emotion is not actually jealousy but the fear of losing someone we love.

Lastly, emotions never stop. You are experiencing emotions right at this minute. You have been having them every moment of your life. We just don't notice them all the time. The bigger emotions get more of our attention, but even in the absence of high drama, we are always emoting.

Practice Session

Close your eyes and notice what you are feeling. It may be a subtle emotion, or it may be something grander. Maybe you are feeling happy or sad. Perhaps you are overwhelmed or relaxed. Just notice. Try this exercise again from time to time and notice how your emotions are always present and always changing.

When we consider emotions as they relate to meditation, we need to remember two important variables. Every emotion, whether based on fear or love, will have these two variables. Once we understand them, we can more easily endure the emotion they relate to.

The first variable is time. All emotions have a basic cycle, meaning they will last for a given amount of time. Granted, some emotions pass quickly while others may last for many years, but all emotions exist in time and are, therefore, temporary. This knowledge can be helpful, both on the meditation cushion and in life.

A while back I met someone very special. He was a wonderful human being, and we made an instant connection. Like many new loves, it started out very intense and ended in a painful breakup. It was very hard to sit with the emotions of that breakup. There were times when I felt I would never feel the same, that I would never feel happiness and peace again. It took everything I had to keep reminding myself that emotions pass.

In time, that pain gave way to compassion and love. In fact, it gave way to a love that was much deeper than anything I could have consciously planned. All emotions are like this. When we are in the middle of them, they feel like the only reality we will ever know, and then they pass on to something else. The schedule is not ours to decide. Emotions run their course in spite of our wishes. There is nothing we can do to change that, except to prolong the pain.

Part of the problem, of course, is that we don't always like the emotions we are feeling; therefore, we want to make them go away. We use any number of techniques to suppress them. Some of us use food to numb out. Others choose sex or drugs. Even some of the new fashionable pharmaceuticals like the antidepressant Prozac are very effective at sweeping our emotions under the rug.

All of these methods have an unfortunate consequence: none are able to shorten the overall amount of time we need to spend with an emotion; they simply act like a pause button. They seem to arrest the emotion, but they only delay the inevitable. Eventually, in this life or in the next, all those emotions will come out. When we learn to sit in meditation, we give those emotions the freedom to release in a healthy and safe way.

The second variable that relates to emotions is their intensity. Not all emotions are created equally. Some emotions may be so subtle that they are barely felt, while others can be so intense they bring us to our knees. All emotions have energy behind them; the only question is how much.

I like to think of the intensity of emotions as being like the wind: sometimes they are a gentle breeze; at other times they have hurricane force. It is always wind, but the varying intensities can be quite a dramatic experience. This is as true of positive emotions as it is of negative ones.

Most of us will have had the experience of being so swept up in love that we could barely move. Conversely, most of us will also have experienced occasions of loss or grief so overwhelming that we could do little more than lie down and cry. Whether the emotion is rooted in love or fear has no bearing on how intense it is. Yet, intensity is another thing we seek to avoid.

When emotions run high, our egos look to escape. Then, many of the tools to which we turn are the same as those we used to avoid the time variable: drugs, sex, food, shopping, and any number of other methods are avoidance tools. Of course, this doesn't diffuse the energy that swells beneath the emotion, so we suppress it and all that energy builds up, just as it would in a pressure cooker.

You may be wondering what all this has to do with meditation, which is, after all, what this book is about. Meditation asks us to sit and stay present, regardless of what comes up. Since we are experiencing emotions all the time, and since these emotions can get intense, they can distract us from our meditation practice. When this happens we need to neutralize them in much the same way as we neutralized the thought patterns and memories that we encountered on the psychological level.

As if all this were not difficult enough, meditation also acts to deepen our awareness of the unconscious. It is in this unconscious level of the mind, as well as in the tissues of the body, that we store all that suppressed emotional energy. Therefore, to sit in meditation is not simply a matter of sitting and noticing the emotions of the moment but it also opens the door for all the suppressed emotions of the past to reveal themselves.

So how do we handle this? If these suppressed emotions were too difficult for us to handle beforehand, why should now be any different? Why should we dig up the past?

These are all very good questions, and they have a simple answer. When we sit and meditate, we deal with emotions in a way that is decidedly different from the way most of us have learned to handle them. Instead of trying to control an emotion, we learn to surrender into it. Seeing emotions like the wind is an apt metaphor. Like the wind, we have no control over what emotions arise. We have no control over how long they will last or even how intense they will be. However, emotions, like the wind, can be a very useful force in our lives and in our meditation practice, too.

Just as we can use the wind to sail and travel great distances, so we can use our emotions to bring us to a deeper understanding of ourselves. Because our emotions have blown most of us around like feathers in the wind, we have learned not to trust their energy. However, through the practice of meditation we can learn to set our sails and let the energy of the emotions take us where we need to go.

How to Meditate When Emotions Arise

As I noted, emotions are bound to arise during your meditation practice. These emotions need to be addressed and not repressed again. In order to do this, we need to remember a few things. First, all emotions will pass. It may take a while—years even—but they will pass. Second, emotions can be very intense. Once we acknowledge this, we are ready to begin.

Let's use an example. Let's say you sit to meditate and the emotion of anger comes up. Sometimes you will have an identifiable target for your anger, such as a boss or co-worker, but in this case let's say it is just a general sense of anger. Because the anger is rather strong, you may be tempted to psychoanalyze it. Or perhaps it is very intense, and you want to avoid it by ending the meditation early or thinking about something more pleasant.

Rather than give in to the above, choose to witness the emotion. Although your pattern may be to escape from the discomfort, choose to sit with the anger this time. Continue returning to the breath or mantra. Remember that emotions are on their own timetable. Remind yourself that the emotions may not go away immediately, but they will surely diminish over time. With this awareness, you won't feel so overwhelmed by them.

Exercise

The next time you are meditating and an emotion arises, don't push it away. Label it (fear, love, joy anger, and so on) and return to the breath. If the emotion continues to distract you, you may want to breathe more slowly and deeply to help keep your mind focused. It is important that you become an observer of the emotion rather than a judge. To let the ego judge and exploit you by creating a new story of its own would be like adding salt to a wound. Continue to acknowledge the emotion while always returning to the breath until the emotion passes, or until your meditation time is complete.

Finding Higher Ground

There are three benefits to working with emotions during a meditation practice. First, we have the opportunity to work through many of the emotions that have been hidden beneath the surface of our consciousness. This allows us to find more emotional balance in our lives and in our relationships, because we lessen the amount of emotional baggage we bring to every situation.

Second, meditation trains the mind to process emotions differently. Even though what we do on the meditation cushion benefits us greatly by freeing the mind from past emotional blocks, we would face an uphill battle if we allowed the emotions to come right back in. Luckily, meditation also teaches us how to process emotions in a healthy way. Thus they fill the mind less and less, and we find a greater sense of stability.

Third, the power that comes from sitting with emotions as they arise allows them to lift us to higher emotional ground. There is a lot of energy behind emotions, and the more intense they are, the more they challenge us. When we learn to ride the wave of energy that underlies all emotions, our threshold for handling emotions is raised. It is not that we feel fewer emotions. We feel the same number as before, but we aren't as easily crushed by them.

Once we find this higher ground, we can begin to make decisions based on logic and inner wisdom rather than the ever-changing tides of our emotional bodies. This leads to a more balanced life and more satisfying relationships, and that is what meditation is all about.

CHAPTER 7

The Group Mind

*Sometimes, during my early-morning meditation, a place with-
in me opens and parts of myself let go that I didn't even know
were holding on. In these moments I feel all the hard places in
my heart and body yield to a great softness carried on my breath,
and I am filled with compassion for the part of me that is always
trying, always organizing, problem solving, anticipating.
My mind stops and simply follows my breath. A great faith
washes through me; a knowing that everything that needs to get
done will get done. My shoulders drop an inch and the small but
familiar ache in my chest eases—the moment stretches.
There is enough: enough time, enough energy, enough of all that
is needed. A great tenderness for myself and the world opens
inside me, and I know that I belong to this time, to these people,
to this earth and to something that is both within and larger
than all of it, something that sustains and holds us all. I do not
want to be anywhere else. I am filled with a commitment to,
and a compassion for myself and the world.*

— *ORIAH MOUNTAIN DREAMER* [1]

Social activism is one topic that my new meditation students bring
up all the time. In general, the people who are interested in self-
improvement through the practice of meditation are also interested in
improving their communities and the world as a whole.

---

1   *The Invitation, 1st edition* by Oriah Mountain Dreamer, HarperOne, April 21,
1999

Because of this, questions inevitably come up around the function of meditation in the healing of our world. It would seem, on the surface anyway, that meditation is nothing more than sitting around doing nothing when there are hungry children to feed and all sorts of other "evils" to address. Let's face it—the world is not a very nice place much of the time. Sitting around watching the breath can feel like denial rather than healing. Understandably, this is a cause for concern for many people.

There are many reasons why meditation can make the world a better place. In fact, in countries where meditation is practiced regularly, the rate of violent crime is significantly lower than in those countries that don't have meditation as part of their culture. The reason for this is multidimensional, and understanding it can be a great help. Therefore, this chapter will focus on some of the basic ways in which an individual meditation practice can help heal our world.

Five Reasons Why Meditation is Good for the World

- When you are more peaceful, you invite others to join in your peace.
- The only thing you can really change is your own mind, but that alone is enough.
- Conflict is always the result of talking louder, rather than becoming still and taking the time to listen.
- Meditation helps you to find happiness. What the world is missing right now is an abundance of genuinely happy people.
- The Unified Field is at the core of all living beings. The degree to which you and I connect with that field affects the whole world—like a ripple in the ocean of life.

The Productive Heart

On the most basic level, meditation enables us to be more focused in our work. We are all called to do different things in this world. I am called to write books, teach yoga and meditation, and so on. Other people are called to be healers, teachers, soldiers, entrepreneurs, and any number of other vocations. These are part of our contribution to the world, but what we are called to do is not what is most significant. One profession or life's work is not more important than another. What is important is the energy we bring to our work.

When I travel to promote my books and teach, I often get comments about my productivity. In addition to teaching in San Francisco, I also teach in other cities around the world. I teach between six and 10 yoga classes per week, and have written and published a number of very successful books.

I write this not to toot my own horn, but rather to demonstrate that meditation doesn't just make me a more peaceful person; it helps me become a more productive person. All of my success in life is, I believe, due to my spiritual practice, which includes seated meditation and yoga. We all have the potential to make our lives incredibly productive. We all have talents and gifts that are very much needed in this world, but distractions abound.

The practice of meditation helps us to organize our thoughts and structure our ideas. Through the practice of meditation, we can open up to the creative flow that is waiting to pour through us, infusing inspiration with passion. Meditation puts the mind in order and brings it under control, opening the door to receive this free flow of perfect energy.

The unfocused mind is like a sledgehammer. The focused mind is like a sharp axe. Both tools can be used to take down a tree, but the axe is going to be much more efficient. Further, using the axe will allow you to work more swiftly, thereby expending much less energy and getting a lot more done.

With the mind sharp, we become more efficient, but it doesn't stop there. As the mind quiets, creativity increases. Our minds are in a natural state of creativity, but the business of our lives clouds that. By taking time to quiet the mind through meditation, we make way for wild creativity that offers a powerful medicine to the world.

I have two friends, Lance and Kathy. Both are exceptional people and are among the most openhearted and compassionate people I know. Few people in this world are able to demonstrate such compassion and grace. In addition, each is an excellent writer with numerous good ideas for books they plan to write.

There is one key difference between them, however. Kathy has a daily meditation practice that she has made an important part of her life. Each morning she gets up, meditates for a half-hour, and then writes for an hour. Of course, this requires she get up a little earlier than she used to do, but the meditation seems to offset her need for extra sleep. Kathy is now publishing her second book.

Lance, on the other hand, still talks and dreams about someday writing a book, but the busy chores of daily life keep him far too distracted to write. As of now, his potential has not been actualized in spite of his open heart and good intentions. It's not simply a loss for Lance; it's a loss for the world.

And so meditation gives us the two things we need most to make a difference in the world: a clear mind and a focused mind. Without these two qualities, even the most open and compassionate person will not have the discipline and structure to manifest their compassion in the world.

The Collective Mind

The benefits of an individual's meditation practice reach far beyond the individual and into the rest of the world. In order to understand the deeper healing that is possible, it is important to understand the collective mind.

Most of us think of the mind as being part of the brain. We also think that the mind is something that begins and ends within an individual's skull. This perception is understandable but unfortunate. Because we tend to understand things in physical terms, we also tend to think of the mind in terms of the primary vehicle through which it is expressed here in the physical realm, i.e., the brain.

The brain is not the mind. This is an important distinction. The mind is something much bigger, and on a very deep level all minds are connected. The mind is the "soul," so to speak. It is expressed through the body, the intellect, and the emotions, but it is none of these. The mind is eternal, infinite, and unified.

This concept has more important consequences in regard to meditation. Because we are all part of one mind, the things I do with my mind have an effect on the collective mind that is shared by all of us. As difficult as this may be to fathom, we are all thinking with the same mind. It is only the ego that tells us we have separate minds. In truth, if you dive deep enough into any two minds, you will see that they meet. I have often heard the collective mind referred to as the ocean. The ocean is one big body of water with many waves on top of it. The waves are connected to each other and the rest of the ocean, yet they seem to be separate. Our minds are much the same way. The collective mind is big and vast like the ocean, and our individual minds are like waves that rise and fall and then return to the ocean.

When we meditate we release old blocks and patterns that are not just our own. We collectively share all sorts of blocks and patterns known as paradigms. In order for a paradigm to shift into a healthier form, the majority of the individual minds involved need to change. This can be a slow process, but it does happen. Our history is filled with paradigm shifts that started off slowly and then, almost overnight the tables were turned. Consider the following passage from my second book, *Yoga and the Path of the Urban Mystic:*

> An example of this can be found in the story of the hundredth monkey, which is actually an illustration of human rather than animal behavior. As the story goes, a scientist was doing an experiment to see how fast a new behavior could be introduced into a tribe of monkeys. The monkeys under study lived on two islands in the south Pacific. Monkeys on both islands were given sweet potatoes to eat each day. These sweet potatoes were not native to the islands, so they were a new experience for the monkeys. According to most accounts, he took one monkey away from the others and taught it how to wash the sweet potatoes in the ocean before eating them.
>
> Then he released the monkey back onto one of the islands and watched to see how long it would take for all the monkeys to develop the new behavior. Gradually, one monkey at a time learned the behavior. It was a slow process at first; but when a certain number of monkeys learned this new behavior (one hundred is the number usually quoted), all the monkeys on the island began to wash their sweet potatoes before eating them. This rapid change in the community's behavior happened almost overnight. The story gets even more amazing, however. At the same time that the scientist was observing the monkeys on the one island, he was also observing the monkeys on the second island nearby, using them as a control group. They were also given sweet potatoes, but none of them were taught

any special behavior. When the hundredth monkey started washing his sweet potatoes on the first island, the monkeys on the second island spontaneously started washing theirs as well.

Subsequent studies[2] have cast doubt on the accuracy of the story as told here. However, its wide acceptance over the years suggests that it illustrates an important tenet of human behavior: our thoughts are available to all other members of our species, though they are free whether or not to think them.

Our history is full of examples of paradigm shifts. We know for certain that there was a time when most, if not all, humans believed the sun revolved around the earth. The idea seemed reasonable to the people of that time because of their limited perspective.

Then came people like Galileo, who had this crazy notion that it was just the opposite. People didn't like this idea very much. They were comfortable with their worldview and didn't appreciate people rocking the boat, so the church exiled him.

Of course, now everyone knows the earth travels around the sun. In fact, if someone were to tell you the opposite, you would consider that person ignorant at best, and probably crazy. Yet, not so many years ago Galileo was ridiculed for questioning that very idea.

We have seen these shifts over and over again throughout history. Movements like woman's suffrage, black civil rights, and the more recent battle over gay civil rights have all begun slowly, started by a few people who opened their minds to new possibilities. In time, when enough people had opened their minds, a nationwide change occurred. Not so long ago, women couldn't vote and African Americans had to sit

---

2   For one such study, visit web page www.context.org/ICLIB/IC09/Myers.htm

in the back of the bus. Now those things are rightly considered unacceptable.

When we sit to meditate, we open our minds and clear away old ideas. In big ways as well as small ways, we are simultaneously clearing out the collective mind. When we do this, we become part of a subtle resonance that heals the whole of humanity.

I like to think of the collective mind as a big pie. Each of us is a piece of that pie. As we meditate, we start to erase those lines that seem to separate us so that we can begin to see the whole rather than the parts.

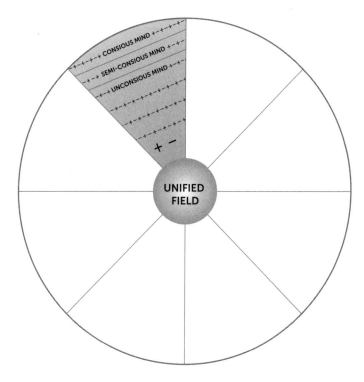

On a more personal level, our meditation practice will directly affect those around us. When I first started meditating and exploring other self-improvement techniques, my family thought I was going nuts. All of a sudden I was no longer playing by the rules that our family had long established. When I started to change my mind about life, my family had two choices. They could change with me or they could live in an awkward state of tension. For the most part, they have learned to grow with me, and in many cases they have inspired me to grow as well.

For example, my father and I get along quite well, but we are very different. Several years ago, I found myself in a relationship with a man. It was quite beautiful, and I decided to share this with my family. I was quite certain that my mother, brother, and sister would handle it well, but I didn't know what to expect from my father.

My father is a great man who would never hurt anyone, but he is very "old school" in his thinking. For him, sexuality and relationships have one primary function: procreation. So telling him that I was in a gay relationship held the potential for disaster.

I spent a lot of time in deep meditation before I told him. I wanted to make sure I was grounded and centered for whatever his reaction would be. I wanted to be at peace, no matter what.

When I told him, he immediately went into lecture mode: "That's just not right!" he exclaimed. "It's just not natural. How are you going to have kids… ?" He continued along those lines for some time. Then I interrupted him.

"Dad, I wasn't asking for your permission. I am in love, and I am happy. You are my father, and I thought you would like to know. I understand if you don't agree with my choices, but it is my life, and I have to do what makes me happy." I was not angry, and I was totally at peace. I truly didn't want to change him, and it must have come across the way I intended.

"Well, it is your life. I just hope that whatever you choose for yourself, you will be happy. That's all any father can hope for his son." With that the subject was changed, and we have not revisited it since. My father is still far from joining PFLAG[3], and he still seems uncomfortable when the subject comes up, but he was changed that day, and so was I. My meditation practice had a domino effect. Rather than take offence and fight and argue with my father, which would have been my previous reaction, I was at peace. This in turn invited him to be at peace, allowing the whole situation to unfold in a more evolved way.

---

3   PFLAG-Parents and friends of Gays and Lesbians · www.pflag.org

Prayer and Meditation

Prayer is talking to God.
Meditation is listening for his answer.
—ALCOHOLICS ANONYMOUS

Although this book is about meditation, I think it is important to mention prayer. While there is a subtle difference between the practice of prayer and the practice of meditation, they are closely related.

I believe that prayer and meditation are really one and the same at their endpoint. Both lead to communion with Spirit and knowledge of our True Nature. Though prayer and meditation can look quite different, they actually complement each other.

The first stage of prayer is what I call desperation mode. This usually happens when we find out that we are in trouble. Perhaps the doctor has just diagnosed you with a serious illness, or maybe your spouse has just asked for a divorce. It is out of the desperation of a life situation that many people turn to prayer. This level of prayer usually sounds something like, "Dear God, my life is a mess. If you fix this mess for me, I promise to be good…"

This, of course, is a good start. Even if it was desperation that brought you to your knees, you are surrendering to something bigger and wiser than yourself. Unfortunately, if your prayer life ends when that crisis is over, another crisis is sure to follow. You can generally count on this cycle being repeated until you are ready for step two. Even at this point though, a meditation practice can be useful, because it helps us to slow down long enough to ask for help.

I think of step two as a major move toward responsibility because it is here that we stop expecting God to mop up the milk we spilled. Instead we ask for a paper towel so we can do it ourselves. A prayer at this level might sound something like "Dear God, I have made a mess of my life. Please show me how to clean up the mess I have created."

It is here that the practice of meditation comes in very handy. It is one thing to ask God for help in learning to clean up whatever mess we've made of our lives, but if we never quiet the mind and listen, how will we know what steps to take? Remember, it was the old thinking that created the mess. A new way of thinking is needed to get things back in order. In Alcoholics Anonymous, they often define insanity as repeating the same action and expecting different results. Quieting the mind is the way we listen for guidance.

The third level of prayer has to do with day-to-day life. In the previous two stages we were praying because life had become uncomfortable. In this third stage we pray proactively. In other words, we turn our minds over to God before the milk even spills. This allows more and more of our life decisions to be made in conjunction with the rest of the universe.

Several weeks ago I was rock climbing with my friends Jasper and Nate. We were at Joshua Tree National Park in southern California. The rocks we were on were a fairly easy climb, so we were not using ropes and other equipment. We easily made it to the top and enjoyed the breath-taking views.

The descent turned out to be more treacherous than we had expected. It was quite steep and virtually impossible to see where to put our hands and feet as we climbed down. For a while, it even felt as if we were going to need to signal for help. Then we decided to be each other's eyes.

As we climbed down, we relied on each other to know where to safely place our feet and hands. At one point, while Jasper was guiding me, I remember feeling a sense of trust. Jasper is one of my closest friends. It was nice to trust him with my life and to have no doubts that he was looking out for me.

Meditation helps us here as well. I needed to listen to Jasper each step of the way. Because of the stakes, my mind was very present to his words, but in the case of prayer, I am not always that present. The practice of meditation makes it much easier to learn to listen to the voice of Spirit guide you through life.

The last stage of prayer is really also the highest form of meditation. Each results in union of the small self with the true Self. Rather than having two wills (the ego and the true Self), we have only one that is in perfect harmony with the rest of the universe. Rather than talking to God and making demands, the practice of prayer and meditation becomes like a perfectly harmonized song that brings with it perfect joy.

Lovingkindness

Every spiritual tradition espouses some form of prayer to benefit others. Buddhists practice *metta*, or lovingkindness. Christians often pray to Jesus, Mother Mary, or various saints on behalf of people in need. Jews have Mi Sheberakh for people who are injured, ill, or in need, and yogis will often turn to their guru for intercession on behalf of a loved one.

Regardless of the tradition, prayer is believed by many to be powerful medicine, and modern science has started to prove what so many hold as an article of faith. It is now well documented that people who are prayed for have better outcomes in surgery and other medical treatments than do those who are not being prayed for. The data even show that this is true regardless of the patient's personal beliefs or whether or not the person is even aware of the prayers.

While offering prayers or positive energy at any time is helpful, doing so when the mind is quiet and the heart is open magnifies the healing effects exponentially. It is for this reason that prayer is particularly effective when offered at the end of a meditation. When the mind is scattered, it is difficult to truly focus the compassionate heart like a laser beam, but when the mind is still, that compassionate heart easily overflows with lovingkindness.

It is also worth noting that the most powerful prayers are not the ones we offer to those who have shown us kindness, but rather to those we perceive as having injured or harmed us in some way. Jesus famously said, "Forgive them, Father, for they know not what they do," as he was being tortured to death. Many would argue that his ability to maintain that peace and equanimity in the face of such brutality is what made his message of forgiveness so powerful.

When we practice forgiveness and lovingkindness as part of our meditation practice, we realize that forgiveness is not just for those who trespass against us. It is first and foremost for ourselves. As the Buddhist master Thich Naht Hanh wrote: "The spring water of the compassionate mind begins to flow, and we ourselves are the first to be cleansed by it. We feel cool and light and we can smile. We do not need two people to bring about reconciliation. When we look deeply, we become reconciled with ourselves and for us, the problem no longer exists. Sooner or later, the other will see our attitude and share in the freshness of the stream of love which is flowing naturally in our heart."

At the end of each of your meditations, take a few moments to bring your awareness to your heart and allow it to open as fully as you are able. As your heart opens, allow yourself to be filled with lovingkindness and compassion. Allow yourself to become so full that your heart expands to encompass all the people you love. Then bring to mind people in need, embracing them with the love a mother shows for her child. Next bring to mind those who have harmed you in some way and offer them the same compassion. Finally, bring to mind the parts of yourself for which you still hold guilt and shame, and allow your compassion to heal yourself as well.

This simple practice is one that will produce great changes in your life and in your relationships. It is a beautiful way for you to practice keeping your heart open while we live in a world that does so much to shut it down.

Buddhist Metta Meditation

The following excerpt is a variation of a traditional Buddhist metta meditation, which was modified by the Buddhist teacher Charlie Day of the Des Moines Meditation and Mindfulness Group [4] following the 9/11 terrorists attacks.

FOR OTHERS

(loved ones, strangers, those in need,
and those that have caused us harm)
May they be well, happy and safe.
May they be free from suffering and at ease with pain.
May they live in peace and harmony with all beings.
May they live with hearts and minds that are always in balance.
May they accept with understanding and wisdom
the events in their lives and world.
May they forgive others and themselves for the inevitable
harms they cause each other.
May they have the patience, courage, understanding,
and determination to overcome the inevitable problems in life.
May they experience and manifest lovingkindness, compassion,
joy and equanimity.

FOR SELF

May I be well, happy and safe.
May I be free from suffering and at ease with pain.
May I live in peace and harmony with all beings.
May I live with a heart and mind that is always in balance.
May I accept with understanding and wisdom
the events in my life and world.

---

4   www.desmoinesmeditation.com

May I forgive others and myself for the inevitable
harms we cause each other.
May I have the patience, courage, understanding,
and determination to overcome the inevitable problems in life.
May I experience and manifest lovingkindness, compassion,
joy and equanimity.

Group Meditation

Intention has everything to do with our experience in meditation. We have already noted the power of the group mind. The phenomenon of the group mind has been well documented, but usually in negative terms.

Take for instance the Holocaust. Hitler was able to convince an otherwise nonviolent people that genocide was acceptable. Most Germans were swept up in the current of false nationalism that resulted in one of the most horrific chapters in human history.

Most of us saw the same principle acted out in high school when classmates formed cliques, then dressed and acted alike. This kind of group energy has great power behind it, and it can move people to focus their energy more deeply for good or for bad.

When we meditate in a group, we are tuning in to the same principle. We are agreeing to sit in stillness with others. It is a simple goal, but because it is shared with others, it can be a very powerful experience.

When I lived in Providence, Rhode Island, my friend Michael and I started a meditation group in our home. Our little group of seven people would meet every Sunday night. We meditated for 30 minutes and then discussed the experience. Even though I was meditating every morning with Michael, there was a noticeable difference in the depths that I was able to reach and how fast the time flew by.

Not only does meditation in a group help deepen one's practice but it also makes a common prayer or intention held by the group more potent. Prayers for people who are sick, or for peaceful resolutions to conflict, are much more effective when a group of people holds the same intention.

In San Francisco, a study conducted by Elizabeth Targ found that the effects of distant healing (various forms of prayer and meditation) notably improved the condition of the patients, who had brain tumors, heart disease or HIV. In the case of distant healing techniques directed to people with HIV, it was found that they were significantly less likely to develop an AIDS-defining illness when they were being prayed for. [5]

Exercise

Gather a group of friends once a week. Meeting in a living room is fine. Agree to sit and meditate for 30 minutes. During the last five minutes of the meditation, hold a common intention for a person or cause you all feel strongly about. Try not to be attached to the outcome. Simply send your good intentions out, and trust they will be received.

Meditation is a powerful personal tool, but the real miracle is how it helps to facilitate healing in the world. Sometimes this healing can be seen and measured, but at other times we have no idea how our personal practice is changing the world.

Whether or not we know the outcomes, meditation is key to healing our own personal sense of dis-ease as well as the conflicts that plague humankind.

It is for this reason that your taking time each day to still the mind is the greatest gift you can offer the world. The universe is a mighty garden. Your job is only to keep your little corner of the garden weeded. Meditation is the tool that allows us to do just that.

---

5   *Health. Hope and HIV by* Stacie Stukin, Yoga Journal
     www.yogajournal.com/health/581

Conclusion

*Only those who partake of the harmony within their souls
know the harmony that runs through nature.
Whosoever lacks this inner harmony
feels also a lack of it in the world.
The mind in chaos finds chaos all around.
How can one know what peace is like
if he has never tasted it?
But he who has inner peace can abide in this state
even in the midst of outer discord.*

—*PARAMAHANSA YOGANANDA*

There was a time in my life when things seemed to happen to me without my having any control over them. Nothing seemed to run smoothly for me. My relationships, work, school, and just about everything else I touched began to rot and decay.

For a while I blamed my parents, society, and even God. I was sure the universe was out to get me and that happiness would always remain an elusive carrot that would keep me running around the racetrack of life until I eventually grew weary and collapsed from chasing it. I pictured myself waiting to be put out to pasture so I could lie down and die.

Then something grand happened. I found the practice of meditation, and I began to live my life. I began to feel happy, and now fulfillment appears in almost every aspect of my day. I still feel pain. Certainly, I have had many difficult times since I began my practice, but those difficulties are less and less able to rob me of my peace of mind.

The other day I was speaking with my mother. Even though we had a rocky time through my teen years, we have grown very close, and I consider her one of my best friends. Shortly after I started meditation, my mother started as well. Once or twice a week we would go to yoga class or to Ellie's meditation group. Meditation was helpful for both of us, and we were growing together.

During this conversation, we were reminiscing about what a special time that was, and how much our lives had changed since. Since starting her meditation practice, my mother has gone back to college, divorced and remarried, started her own business, and traveled around the country with her new husband.

More importantly, she is free.

"Darren, meditation has been such a gift," she told me. "I felt so stuck before. It wasn't that my life was awful. I just wasn't happy. There was so much I wanted to do but could not seem to find the courage to move my feet. I knew I wasn't happy but couldn't seem to find a way to make the changes."

"Once I started meditating," she continued, "things opened up for me. I started to think outside the lines, and all the energy I used to put into letting the neighbors think I was happy went into actually finding happiness for myself. I don't know what the future holds for me. I don't know what decisions I will need to make tomorrow, but I do know this—I will never allow myself to feel trapped again. I now know that all I have to do is sit and be still. When I do that, all the pieces of my life come together."

My mother is such a wise woman. She has dedicated her life to her children, and I am so grateful that meditation has brought her the personal happiness that she has offered to so many others. The good news is that she and I are not alone. Anyone can find the peace that thousands of people around the world have found, simply by taking time each day to sit still, quiet the mind and listen.

When we do this, the rewards are countless and profound. From the physical benefits, such as reduced blood pressure and increased immunity, to the emotional benefits, such as a more balanced emotional state, meditation delivers its rewards quickly and without prejudice. You can be young or old, black or white, religious or atheist, cynical or naive. Meditation offers us an open mind and an open heart, and it helps us to heal ourselves and our world on every level.

Meditation is work, however, and to practice it consistently takes discipline and commitment. The ego mind will do everything it can to keep you busy, but in the end, all the ego's searching will only leave you feeling empty. In contrast, for all the hard work that meditation presents us, it also offers rewards that fill us from the inside by helping us to realize we are whole and complete to begin with.

And so I leave you with this thought. Look at all the things in your life. None of them mean anything without a quiet mind and a peaceful heart. Even our closest relationships will be strained if we come to them without first looking within. Therefore, make a commitment to seek peace within each day. It doesn't have to be hours. Twenty to 30 minutes will make all the difference. But give yourself and the world this stillness.

The time in my life when I felt like a victim has passed, thanks to meditation. I now make my own choices. They are not always wise choices, but at least they are mine, and if I don't like the outcome, I can choose again until I get it right. Through meditation everyone can take the wheel of his or her own life and choose peace.

May all beings be happy.
May all beings be at peace.
Om Shanti.

Frequently Asked Questions

*Meditation is universally feasible because every human
being is contemplative by nature. In fact, we are
unknowingly practicing meditation while standing,
sitting, lying, walking, eating, drinking, and speaking.
There is not a single moment when we are not meditating.
It could be said that meditation is our profession,
but even at night we continue meditating in our dreams.
But like many other things, we do not adopt the conscious
practice of meditation for lack of interest, or at best
we practice haphazardly. While haphazard efforts at
meditation never go to waste, practicing meditation
regularly and systematically brings pleasant and
mysterious experiences, increasing one's faith day by day.*

—SWAMI KRIPALU

How often should I meditate? How long should I meditate?

The nice thing about meditation is that you cannot meditate too much.
I recommend a daily practice of 20 to 30 minutes. I would choose a
consistent time each day and make it a regular part of your daily routine. The important thing is to be consistent with your practice.

How do I know when my time is up?

Knowing when it is time to end your meditation will get easier with
practice. The more you meditate, the easier it will be for you to know
how much time has passed. In the meantime you can take a watch and

place it on the floor in front of you. Be sure to check the time when you start and make a mental note of when your time will be over. That will save you having to do the math when you check. Here are a few tips:

- Use a watch or clock that is easy to read.
- Do the math ahead of time.
- If you choose to use some sort of alarm, make sure it has a soothing sound. To support you in this, you can easily download my guided meditation CD from Amazon. com or from iTunes. You can also use a program like the "Meditator" application for the iPhone to guide your meditations.

REMEMBER: Never end your meditation early. If you do, you will start a very bad habit.

When is the best time to meditate?

There is no wrong time to meditate. There are, however, times that will be more difficult than others. Personally, I like to start my day with a meditation, but some find that meditating at other times of the day works better for them. The key is to find a time each day when you can sit. Here are a few other tips:

- Meditate at the same time each day.
- Avoid meditation just after a large meal.
- Use the ego's need for habit to your advantage to create a healthy pattern with your practice.
- Avoid meditation just before bedtime, as you may be sleepy.
- Try making time to meditate twice a day.

Will meditation interfere with my religion?

The practice of meditation is not a religion. A religion is a belief system that some people believe in and others do not. Meditation is a practice that doesn't require belief in God or anything else. It can, however, be a great way to deepen one's religion.

Some religions oppose meditation. Usually this has more to do with fear and lack of understanding than religious conviction. If you feel that there is a conflict between your meditation practice and your religion, you may want to find a meditation technique that is rooted in your religious tradition.

Should I listen to music?

I don't listen to music when I meditate. Other people find it helpful. This is something you will need to explore for yourself. On the one hand the music may be a noise distraction, but on the other hand we live in a noisy world. The music may give you some sense of control over what kind of noise works best for you while you practice.

What happens when I miss a day?

Missing a day is not the end of the world. However, it is important that you are very careful not to let a pattern develop. Your strong intention should be to make meditation a daily practice. If you miss a day, don't beat yourself up. Rather, reaffirm your commitment to the practice and make sure you meditate as soon as possible.

Even if you miss a whole week or month, don't beat yourself up. Simply return to your practice and try to make sure you don't let yourself forget the importance of the practice. Just like you return to the breath, return to the practice because that is where growth happens.

My body hurts when I sit. What can I do about this?

In the West we are used to sitting in chairs. Sitting on the floor is not going to be easy at first, and accepting a certain amount of discomfort may be necessary. Here are a few other tips for making your body more comfortable in your practice:

- Invest in a good meditation cushion or pad. *(See Appendix C.)*
- Consider sitting in a straight-backed chair with your feet on the floor.
- Take hatha yoga classes regularly to help your body become more flexible.
- Stretch out your legs and hips before you sit to meditate.
- Use folded blankets to support your knees.

No matter how hard I try, I keep getting distracted.
What's wrong with me?

Getting distracted is part of the practice. Your mind will wander. Count on it and expect it, BUT don't cater to it. If the mind gets distracted a thousand times during a sit, bring it back to the breath a thousand and one times. Meditation is not about avoiding distraction; it is about returning to the breath (or another point of focus) over and over again. It is the return from distraction that frees the mind and gives us control.

Styles of Meditation

Style	Tradition	Website
Vipassana (S.N. Goenka)	Buddhist	www.dhamma.org
Vipassana (Insight)	Buddhist	www.dharma.org
Centering Prayer	Christian	www.centeringprayer.com
Kabbalah Meditation	Jewish	www.kabbalahmeditation.org
Sufi Heart Meditation	Islam	www.goldensufi.org
Transcendental Meditation (TM)	Yogic	www.tm.org
Hong Sau	Yogic	www.yogananda-sfr.org

Meditation Props
and Supplies

Those who know are silent.
Those who do not, babble on forever.
Surrender your demands.
Forego your dreams. Ignore magical tricks.
Abandon the marketplace.
Claim neither victory nor defeat.
Feel the earth living in muscle and blood.
Spoken it loses its meaning.
Lived its power transcends limitation.

—*HAVEN TREVINO, THE TAO OF HEALING*

Company	Phone	Website
Yoga Props	888-856-9642	www.yogaprops.net
Dharma Crafts	800-794-9862	www.dharmacrafts.com
GAIAM	877-989-6321	www.gaiam.com
Hugger Mugger	800-473-4888	www.huggermugger.com
The British Wheel of Yoga (Europe)	0138-6859553	www.bwy-shop.co.uk

Acknowledgments

Special thanks to my family

My mother, Kathy Ascare; my father, John Main; my brother, Jason Main; my sister, Jennifer Main-Holdridge; my nieces, Zoe Main, Haley Joe Holdridge, and Lauren Glaza; and my nephews, Chase, Jake, and Tyler Flynn. Also to the Mains and Flynns: Don, Amy, Alden, Josie, Joe, John, Sarah, Peter, Linda, Kate, Gus, Adelina, Arthur, and Mary, and all the others who are too numerous to mention.

Special thanks to the many friends
who have supported me so much:

Lance King, Michael Lynch, Christopher Love, Jasper Trout, Keir Lee, Michael Watson, Sue Louiseau, Kevin Hicks, Wanda Pierce, Brian Lyttle, Tim and Tara Dale, Kimberly Wilson, Michael Alexander, Anoop Badola, Katherine Chapman, Sam Jackson, Jamie Lindsay, Christine Maggiore, Robin Scovill, Ryan Brewer and Bodhi Maisha

To my editors

Sue Louiseau and Peter Wong—Thank you so much for your tireless efforts in editing my words in this book and in everything I write. You both have the patience of a saint to be able to deal with my spelling!

I would also like to thank my editing team: Teresa Pasahow, KayDee Kersten, Elliot Bringman, Brennan Taylor, Vanessa Wilcox, Kartik Shah, Mags Aleks, LeAnne Berry, Katie Bowser, Deanna Pinkston, Angie Ryan, Amy Khan, Gregory Johnson, and Ellyn Shea.

Special thanks to Jasper Trout for creating such a beautiful cover for this book.

I would also like to thank Thierry Bogliolo and all the staff at Findhorn Press. Without their faith in my writing, none of my books would have been possible.

Choosing to Be

Lessons in Living from
a Feline Zen Master

by Kat Tansey

Beginning meditators are urged to first find a teacher. But what if that teacher is already close at hand, living under the same roof, has four legs, wears a fur coat, and quietly embodies a Bodhisattva? In this charming and insightful story, former businesswoman Kat Tansey reveals how her Maine Coon cat Poohbear and his young cohort Catzenbear pulled her back from the brink of illness and depression through a series of life lessons rooted in the timeless wisdom of the feline world and the Buddha. Over time, as the author learns to slow down, accept each moment as it comes, and enjoy life again, her deepening meditation practice becomes a path back to the human world and retreats with Insight Meditation teacher Jason Siff, whose down-to-earth teaching style and inquiry method perfectly complement kitty wisdom. Anyone who struggles or has struggled with life's many challenges will relate to this humorous tale illustrating the joys and comforts of answering to a cat master.

ISBN 978-1-84409-501-8

FINDHORN PRESS

Life Changing Books

For a complete catalogue,
please contact:

Findhorn Press Ltd
117-121 High Street,
Forres IV36 1AB,
Scotland, UK

t +44 (0)1309 690582
f +44 (0)131 777 2711
e info@findhornpress.com

or consult our catalogue online
(with secure order facility) on
www.findhornpress.com

For information on the Findhorn Foundation:
www.findhorn.org